'SPECIFIC RELIEF ACT 1963' - SUPREME COURT'S LATEST CASE LAWS

CASE NOTES- FACTS- FINDINGS OF APEX COURT JUDGES & CITATIONS

JAYPRAKASH BANSILAL SOMANI

Dedicated

To

All the Past & Present Judges of the Supreme Court of India.

Salute to their wisdom.

Salute to their interpretation of Law.

Salute to their elaborative judgement writing.

SUPREME COURT OF INDIA

Contents

Contents

Preface

Dear Learned Advocates of Trial Court, High court and Supreme Court, Corporate and Individuals.

I am very delighted to provide you a book on 'SPECIFIC RELIEF ACT 1963'- SUPREME COURT'S LATEST LEADING CASE LAWs

In this book you will get...

1. Name of the Case i. e. Cause title

2.Relevant Sections discussed in the case

3. Hon'ble Judges/Coram of the case

4.Number of PDF Pages in Original Judgement of the case

5. All available Citations of the case

6. Case Note with appeal allowed/ dismissed or disposed off

7. Facts of the case

8. Hon'ble Apex Court's findings, while dismissing/allowing or disposing the appeal

9. Ratio Decidendi if any.

My special thanks to Manupatra, because of their web portal I can compile this book in well manner. I am also thankful to Notion Press to support me to publish & market this book throughout the Country. Thanks to my Juniors, Advocate Colleagues & Insolvency Professional Colleagues to support me in this venture.

Adv. Manoj Kumar Chowdhary & Adv. Shruti Kriti has helped me a lot to compile this book. I hope this book will add some value addition in the wealth of your legal knowledge. Your positive feedbacks will boost me to compile/ write further books & negative feedbacks will improve my skills. Kindly send your valuable feedbacks by email.

Thanks with Regards,

Jayprakash B. Somani

Advocate, Supreme Court of India

Email: jaysomani64@gmail.com

Web Site: www.jayprakashsomani.com

Call: 9322188701, 8459194576

Acknowledgements

Printed & Published by
Notion Press
No. 8, 3rd Cross Street,
CIT Colony, Mylapore,
Chennai, Tamil Nadu- 600004

• • •

Managed by
Jayprakash Somani Advocates & Solicitors
Law Firm for Supreme Court of India
Delhi Office
B- 851, 1st Floor, Shivaji Marg, New Ashok Nagar, Delhi 110096.
Call: 9322188701, 8459194576
Supreme Court Chamber
312, 3rd Floor, M. C. Setalvad Block, In front of 'D' Gate, Bhagwan Das
Road, Supreme Court of India, New Delhi 110001
Contact: 8459194576, 9811011747
www.jayprakashsomani.com

• • •

Download our app to get access to our Free Videos, Free Bare Acts,
Free Study Material in Legal as well as International Business Regime.
Android App Link ;-https://clpandrea.page.link/cmSm
Ios APp Link :-https://apps.apple.com/us/app/classplus/ld1324522260
Login with org code ;- (qywzji)
Web Link ;-https://qywzji.courses.store/
Opportunity for Lawyers/ Social Workers to get Supreme Court Law
Firm JSAS's authorised centre at District Level.
Kindly Message or Call to: 9322188701

• • •

Books are available online in India
1. **Notion Press:**https://notionpress.com/author/jayprakash_somani
2. **Amazon:**https://www.amazon.in/s?k=jayprakash+somani
3. **Flipkart:**https://www.flipkart.com/search?q=Jayprakash%20Somani

Books are available online at International Market
4. Amazon International: https://www.amazon.com/
s?k=jayprakash+somani
5. Amazon United Kingdom: https://www.amazon.co.uk/
s?k=jayprakash+somani
6. E-Books/Kindle edition at National & International Level:
https://www.amazon.in/s?k=jaypraksh+somani

• • •

C. Haridasan vs. Anappath Parakkattu Vasudeva Kurup and Ors. (13.01.2023 – SC) : MANU/SC/0031/2023

Relative Section:

Constitution of India - Article 142;

Kerala Land Reforms Act, 1963;

Specific Relief (Amendment) Act, 2018;

Specific Relief Act 1963 - Section 10, Section 10(a), Section 11, Section 11(2,Section 14,Section 16, Section 16(c), Section 20, Section 20(2)

Hon'ble Judges/Coram: B.V. Nagarathna and M.R. Shah, JJ.

Equivalent Citation:

2023(1)ALD259, 2023(1)ALD259, 2023(1)CTC605, 2023/INSC/32, 2023(1)KLJ532, (2023)1MLJ578, 2023 (1) MWN 664

Number of Pages in the Original Judgment:23

Case Reference:

Pratap Lakshman Muchandi and Ors. v. Shamlal Uddavadas Wadhwa and Ors. MANU/SC/7078/2008; Mehboob-Ur-Rehman (Dead) through L.Rs. v. Ahsanul Ghani MANU/SC/0218/2019; Sughar Singh v. Hari Singh (Dead) through L.Rs. and Ors. MANU/SC/0985/2021; Bachhaj Nahar v. Nilima Mandal and Ors. MANU/SC/8199/2008; Motilal Jain v. Ramdasi Devi and Ors. MANU/SC/0438/2000; Syed Dastagir v. T.R. Gopalakrishnasetty MANU/SC/0471/1999; Acharya Swami Ganesh Dassji v. Sita Ram Thapar MANU/SC/0522/1996; J.P. Builders and Ors. v. A. Ramadas Rao and Ors. MANU/SC/0977/2010; Saradamani Kandappan and Ors. v. S. Rajalakshmi and Ors. MANU/SC/0717/2011; K.S. Vidyanadam and Ors. v. Vairavan MANU/SC/0404/1997; B. Santoshamma v. D. Sarala and Anr. MANU/SC/0698/2020 : (2020) 19 SCC 80; Shenbagam v. K.K. Rathinavel MANU/SCOR/08297/2022

Case Note:

Contract - Specific performance - Readiness and willingness - Section 16(c) Specific Relief Act, 1963 - Plaintiff and Defendants entered into agreement to sell under which Defendants agreed to sell land for consideration - Plaintiff paid amount as advance towards part sale consideration amount - Thereafter, Plaintiff served legal notice upon Defendants to execute sale deed to which Defendants refused to execute agreement and cancelled agreement to sell - Therefore, Appellant-original Plaintiff instituted suit before Trial Court for specific performance of agreement to sell - Trial Court decreed suit for specific performance of agreement to sell and also directed Plaintiff to pay twenty five percent more amount, over and above agreed consideration- In appeal, High Court opined that trial Court was not justified in enhancing sale consideration and ought not to have exercised discretion in favour of Plaintiff - High Court had set aside judgment and decree for specific performance - Hence, present appeal - Whether Plaintiff's conduct demonstrates readiness and willingness on his part to carry out his obligations under agreement of sale.

Facts:

The Plaintiff and the Defendants entered into an agreement to sellunder which the Defendants agreed to sell the land in question for a consideration. The Plaintiff paid an amount as advance towards the part sale consideration amount. The balance consideration was agreed to be paid by the Plaintiff within six months from the date after measuring the property provided the Defendants make available the documents of title including the purchase certificate under the Kerala Land Reforms Act.That thereafter, the Plaintiff served a legal notice upon the Defendants to execute the sale deed to which the Defendants sent reply and refused to execute the sale deed and cancelled the agreement to sell. Therefore, the Appellant - original Plaintiff instituted a Suit for specific performance of agreement to sell and in the alternative return of thePlaintiff's amount with interest.On appreciation of the entire evidence on record, the trial Court decreed the suit for specific performance of agreement to sell. However, at the same time and to do complete justice between the parties, the trial Court directed the Plaintiff to pay twenty five percent more amount, over and above the agreed consideration. In appeal, the High Court opined that the trial Court was not justified in enhancing the sale consideration and ought not to have exercised the discretion in favour of the Plaintiff. The High Court had set aside the judgment and decree for specific performance and had directed the Defendants to pay sum to the Plaintiff.

Held, while disposing off the appeal:

M.R. Shah, J.

(i) When to do the complete justice and relying upon and considering the decision of this Court in the case of Pratap Lakshman Muchandi v.

ShamlalUddavadas Wadhwa, the trial Court directed the Plaintiff to pay some more amount than the amount mentioned in the agreement to sell, at the most, the Plaintiff can be said to be aggrieved. Still, the High Court had considered such an order passed by the trial Court against the Defendants. As such, the trial Court was absolutely justified in compensating the Defendants by paying some more amount while passing a decree for specific performance. Therefore, in the facts and circumstances of the case and more particularly when the trial Court exercised the discretion in favour of the Plaintiff after having observed and recorded the findings on the execution of the agreement to sell by the Defendants and that the part sale consideration was paid by the Plaintiff which was accepted by the Defendants and thereafter the finding that the Plaintiff was always ready and willing to perform his part of the contract, the trial Court was absolutely justified in passing the decree for specific performance. The High Court had erred in interfering with the judgment and decree passed by the trial Court, without setting aside the findings recorded by the trial Court recorded while passing the decree for specific performance. The impugned judgment and order passed by the High Court was unsustainable, both, on law as well as on facts. [7]

B.V. Nagarathna, J.

(i) It was an admitted fact that the Plaintiff had paid an amount, which constituted merely four percent of the consideration. The Trial Court itself recorded findings to the effect that neither party had initiated timely steps to perform their respective obligations under the contract. Although the Defendants did not make available the title deeds of the Schedule property to the Plaintiff, it could not be said that the conduct of the Defendants had prevented the Plaintiff from tendering the balance sale consideration, within the stipulated date, or at any time before filing the suit for specific performance as the whole object of the intended sale was to garner funds for discharging a debt which was ultimately done by the Defendants by selling family jewellery. [36]

(ii) The Trial Court's judgment records a finding to the effect that the Defendants had applied for the purchase certificate in the year, i.e., soon after entering into the agreement of sale of Kanam and Kuzhikoor rights. This fact would suggest that there was no delay on the part of the Defendant in acting in pursuance of the agreement. The fact that the purchase certificate was granted by the concerned authority, was beyond the control of the Defendants and such delay could not be attributed to the Defendants.

The Defendants had duly initiated the process of obtaining a purchase certificate soon after entering into the agreement. [37]

(iii) The Plaintiff in the present case served a legal notice while the six month period stipulated in the agreement had elapsed. There was no explanation as to what occasioned the delay in serving the legal notice on the Defendants and why such steps were not adopted soon after the expiry of the six month period stipulated in the agreement of sale of Kanam and Kuzhikoor rights. [42]

(iv) The conduct of the Plaintiff was not reflective of his readiness as well as willingness on his part to pursue the agreement of sale of Kanam and Kuzhikoor rights, in terms of Section 16(c) of the Act. [45]

• • •

CHAPTER II

Desh Raj and Ors. vs. Rohtash Singh (14.12.2022 – SC) : MANU / SC/1615/2022

Relative Section:

Code of Civil Procedure, 1908 (CPC) - Section 100; Haryana Development And Regulation Of Urban Areas Act, 1975 - Section 2(o), Haryana Development And Regulation Of Urban Areas Act, 1975 - Section 7A; Hindu Minority and Guardianship Act, 1956; Indian Contract Act, 1872 - Section 55, Indian Contract Act, 1872 - Section 74; Land Acquisition Act, 1894 - Section 4; Specific Relief Act 1963 - Section 22, Specific Relief Act 1963 - Section 22(1), Specific Relief Act 1963 - Section 22(2)

Hon'ble Judges/Coram: Surya Kant and Bela M. Trivedi, JJ.

Equivalent Citation:

2023(243)AIC22, AIR2023SC163, 2023(1)ALD124, 2023 (158) ALR 190, 2023(1)ALT36, 2023 3 AWC2161SC, 2023(1)BLJ176, 2022 (4) CCC 348 , 2023(2)CGLJ23, 2023(1)CivilCC(S.C.), 2023(1)CTC348, 2023GLH(1)29, 2023(1)ICC988, 2022/INSC/1277, 2023(1)KLJ371, 2023(1)KLT347, 2023 (1) MWN 403, 2023(I)OLR55, 2023(1)RCR(Civil)334, 2023 160 RD279, (2023)3SCC714

Number of Pages in the Original Judgment: 15

Case Reference:

K.S. Vidyanadam and Ors. v. Vairavan MANU/SC/0404/1997; Satish Batra v. Sudhir Rawal MANU/SC/0887/2012; Fateh Chand v. Balkishan Das MANU/SC/0258/1963; Saradamani Kandappan and Ors. v. S. Rajalakshmi and Ors. MANU/SC/0717/2011; Kailash Nath Associates v. Delhi Development Authority MANU/SC/0019/2015; Oil & Natural Gas Corporation Ltd. v. SAW Pipes Ltd. MANU/SC/0314/2003; Rohatash Singh v. Deshraj SLP (Civil) No. 11901 of 2022; Citadel Fine Pharmaceuticals v. Ramaniyam Real Estates Private Ltd. MANU/SC/0939/2011 : (2011) 9 SCC 147

Case Note:

Contract - Performance of Contractual Obligations - Section 74 of Contract Act, 1872; Section 22 of the Specific Relief Act of 1963 ('SRA Act') - Present appeal is directed against the judgment passed by the High

Court whereby a second appeal preferred by the Appellants was dismissed and judgment and decree of the Trial Court as well as the First Appellate Court were affirmed, the decree entitled the Respondent for the recovery of earnest money, which constituted of partly paid sale consideration in lieu of the concerned agreements to sale along with requisite interest - Whether Time was the Essence of the Contract and whether that it was Proved that Appellants were willfully Avoiding Performance of Their Contractual Obligations and that whether Respondent was Entitled to recovery of earnest money?

Facts:

The Trial Court concluded that both the parties were equally responsible for rendering the Sale Agreements as unenforceable. While it hesitantly accepted the stance of both the parties in respect to the contention that they were present before the Sub-Registrar on the Date of Execution, it held that the same was meaningless as the Appellants were at fault for not taking effective steps in procuring the NOC Under Section 7A of Haryana Development and Regulation of Urban Areas Act of 1975 ('HUDA Act').However, the Trial Court then went on to hold that the Sale Agreements were either way rendered impossible to perform in view of the land acquisition proceedings and proceeded to grant decree of recovery of earnest money on the principle of unjust enrichment. The First Appellate Court upheld the decree granted by Trial Court on entirely identical reasons. The High Court in its impugned judgment made two observations which are pertinent to note - first that no evidence was led by the parties to prove whether they took requisite steps to obtain the NOC Under Section 7A of HUDA Act and; second that presence of Appellants before the Sub-Registrar on 31.08.2004 or 01.09.2004 when last opportunity to execute the sale deed was granted to Respondent, was doubtful as the evidence of marking their presence was not proved and that legal notices dated 18.08.2004 were not served on the Respondent. The High Court, thus, went on to uphold the decree passed by the courts below, noting that in view of the acquisition proceedings, the alternate relief of recovery of earnest money was legally correct. The aggrieved Appellants are before this Court.

Held, while allowing the appeal

1. Throughout the entire dispute, Appellants have taken a consistent stand of time-bound performance being an essence of the contract. They have maintained that sale deed was needed to be executed necessarily on the Date of Execution as agreed between the parties. It is unfortunate that

all the courts below have failed to render a finding on this aspect despite the fact that this was one of the key defenses taken by the Appellants in respect of the prayer seeking specific performance. [20]

2. The Sale Agreements in the present case clearly indicate the intention of the parties to treat time-bound performance as an essential condition. They stipulate that in case the sale deed was not executed on the Date of Execution, the Sale Agreements were liable to be treated as cancelled, and the earnest money was to be forfeited. Even in the legal notices dated 18.08.2004, through which last opportunity was extended to Respondent to execute the sale deed, the factum of time being an essential condition for performance was reiterated. On the other hand, no evidence or communication has been brought on record by the Respondent to contradict the defense of time-bound performance taken by the Appellants. [22]

3. Present Court must shift attention to the High Court's observation that the presence of Appellants before the Sub-Registrar was doubtful on 31.08.2004 and 02.09.2004 as the affidavits of their presence were not proved in the evidence. In contrast, the Trial Court has found that these affidavits were duly proved in the cross examination of the Appellants and the said finding of fact was affirmed by the First Appellate Court. The High Court, therefore, ought not to have made any fact based observations especially when the records of the courts below were not requisitioned to reach an independent conclusion to hold that the said finding of fact by the two courts was contrary to the record. The re-appreciation of evidence is ordinarily impermissible and beyond the scope of a second appeal. Even otherwise, the presence of Appellants before the Sub-Registrar on the Date of Execution is not disputed. [29]

4. Section 22 of the Specific Relief Act of 1963 ('SRA Act') which provides that any person suing for the specific performance of the contract for the transfer of property may ask for - (a) possession or partition and separate possession of the property in addition of such performance OR (b) such person may seek any other relief to which he is entitled to "including the refund of any earnest money or deposit paid or made by him" in case his claim for specific performance is refused. However, Sub-section (2) thereof puts a caveat that the abovementioned reliefs shall not be granted by the court unless "it has been specifically claimed". The proviso to Sub-section (2) further says that even if such relief was not specifically claimed in the plaint, it is the discretion of the Court to permit the Plaintiff to amend the

plaint "at any stage of the proceedings" and allow him to include the claim for refund of the earnest money or deposit paid.the Plaintiff in his suit for specific performance of a contact is not only entitled to seek specific performance of the contract for the transfer of immovable property but he can also seek alternative relief(s) including the refund of any earnest money, provided that such a relief has been specifically incorporated in the plaint. The court, however, has been vested with wide judicial discretion to permit the Plaintiff to amend the plaint even at a later stage of the proceedings and seek the alternative relief of refund of the earnest money. The litmus test appears to be that unless a Plaintiff specifically seeks the refund of the earnest money at the time of filing of the suit or by way of amendment, no such relief can be granted to him. The prayer Clause is a sine qua non for grant of decree of refund of earnest money. [31]

5. The Respondent in the instant case has neither pleaded for refund of the earnest money nor has he claimed any damages or penalty from the Appellants. From the perusal of the records, it is conspicuous that Respondent never raised any concern that the pre estimated amount was 'penal' in nature and instead his sole objective was to gain titular rights over the Concerned Property on the strength of Sale Agreements. [36]

6. The decree granted by the courts below was hinged on a logical fallacy wherein the Appellants were held to be unjustly enriched on the premise that the contract was rendered impossible to perform due to acquisition proceedings. On the contrary, the contract automatically stood terminated as per the stipulated contractual terms. The Sale Agreements should have been rightly held to be terminated instead of being declared impossible to perform. [37]

. Furthermore, present Court deem it appropriate to hold that, the forfeiture was justified and within the confines of reasonable compensation as per Section 74 of Contract Act in light of the fact that during the entirety of proceedings - firstly the nature of forfeiture was never contested by the Respondent and secondly the Respondent never prayed for the refund of earnest money. Consequently, the judgments rendered by the Courts below deserve to be set aside and the suit is liable to be dismissed. [38]

8. Appeal allowed. [39]

Ratio Decidendi: Unless a Plaintiff specifically seeks the refund of the earnest money at the time of filing of the suit or by way of amendment, no such relief can be granted to him

Disposition: Appeal Allowed

• • •

P. Daivasigamani vs. S. Sambandan (12.10.2022 – SC) : MANU/ SC / 1309/2022

Relative Section:

Limitation Act, 1963 - Schedule - Article 54; Specific Relief (Amendment) Act, 2018; Specific Relief Act 1963 - Section 10, Specific Relief Act 1963 - Section 16, Specific Relief Act 1963 - Section 16(c), Specific Relief Act 1963 - Section 20, Specific Relief Act 1963 - Section 20(2), Specific Relief Act 1963 - Section 21, Specific Relief Act 1963 - Section 22, Specific Relief Act 1963 - Section 23, Specific Relief Act 1963 - Section 24

Hon'ble Judges/Coram: Sanjiv Khanna and Bela M. Trivedi, JJ.

Equivalent Citation:

2022(240)AIC1, AIR2022SC5009, 2023(1)ALD49, 2023 (156) ALR 218, 2022 (4) CCC 358 , 2023(1)Civil CC (S.C.), 2023(1)ICC775, 2022/INSC/ 1068, 2022(4)RCR(Civil)497, 2023 158 RD612, 2022(Suppl.)Sim.L.C.272

Number of Pages in the Original Judgment: 12

Case Reference:

Madamsetty Satyanarayana v. G. Yellogi Rao and Ors. MANU/SC/0310/ 1964; R. Lakshmikantham v. Devaraji MANU/SC/0969/2019; Syed Dastagir v. T.R. Gopalakrishnasetty MANU/SC/0471/1999; Sukhbir Singh and Ors. v. Brij Pal Singh and Ors. MANU/SC/0629/1996; A. Kanthamani v. Nasreen Ahmed MANU/ SC 0234/2017; C.S. Venkatesh v. A.S.C. Murthy (D) by L.Rs. and Ors. MANU/SC/0142/2020; Kamal Kumar v. Premlata Joshi and Ors. MANU/SC/0012/2019; Ritu Saxena v. J.S. Grover and Ors. MANU/SC/1279/2019; Abdullakoya Haji and Ors. v. Rubis Tharayil and Ors. MANU/SC/1120/2019; Acharya Swami Ganesh Dassji v. Sita Ram Thapar MANU/SC/0522/1996; N.P. Thirugnanam (D) by L.Rs., v. R. Jagan Mohan Rao and Ors. MANU/SC/0025/1996; Ardeshir H. Mama v. Flora Sassoon MANU/PR/0149/1928; K.S. Vidyanadam and Ors. v. Vairavan MANU/SC/0404/1997; Saradamani Kandappan and Ors. v. S. Rajalakshmi and Ors. MANU /SC/0717/2011; Smt. Katta Sujatha Reddy v. Siddamsetty Infra Projects Ltd. Civil Appeal No. 5822 of 2022

Case Note:

Contract - Specific performance - Readiness and willingness - Section 16(c) of Specific Relief Act, 1963 - Respondent-Plaintiff had filed suit in Trial Court seeking specific performance of agreement for sale against Appellant-Defendant and had prayed in alternative for refund of earnest (advance) money with interest, and also for compensation - Respondent had also prayed for permanent injunction restraining Appellant from alienating or transferring suit property - Trial Court partly decreed suit granting prayer for refund of earnest money with interest and dismissed suit so far as other prayers were concerned - Trial Court held that Plaintiff had failed to prove his readiness and willingness to perform his part of agreement - In appeal, High Court decreed suit of Respondent-Plaintiff - Hence, present appeal - Whether High Court was justified in granting relief of specific performance by holding that Respondent-Plaintiff had proved readiness and willingness on his part.

Facts:

The Respondent (original Plaintiff) had filed the suit in the Trial Court seeking specific performance of an agreement for sale against the Appellant (original Defendant) and had prayed in the alternative for refund of the earnest (advance) money with interest, and also for the compensation. The Respondent had also prayed for permanent injunction restraining the Appellant-Defendant from alienating or transferring the suit property to any third party. The Trial Court partly decreed the suit granting prayer for refund of the earnest money with interest and dismissed the suit so far as other prayers were concerned, vide the judgment and decree. The Trial Court, therefore, came to the conclusion that the Plaintiff had failed to prove his readiness and willingness to perform his part of the agreement, and therefore was not entitled to the decree for specific performance of the agreement, however he was entitled to recover from the Defendant the amount paid by way of advance, together with interest. The High Court in the appeal, decreed the suit of the Respondent-Plaintiff. The High Court come to the conclusion that the finding of the Court below to the effect that the Appellant/Plaintiff had not proved his continued readiness and willingness to perform his part of the obligations under the agreement was not based on sound reasoning and in fact it was perverse finding, which deserves interference by this Court. It was held that the Appellant/Plaintiff has complied with the requirements of Section 16(c) of the SpecificRelief Act by making a specific pleading regarding his readiness and willingness and proving the same by reliable evidence.

Held, while dismissing the appeal:

(i) The Respondent-Plaintiff had not only averred in the plaint about his issuing notices within the period of six months of the agreement in question, calling upon the Appellant-Defendant to perform his part of contract and conclude the sale transaction, also showing his readiness and willingness to perform his part of the contract, but the Respondent had also proved the same by stepping into the witness box. Though much reliance was placed by the Appellant on the decisions of this Court in case of Ritu Saxena v. J.S. Grover and Anr, in case of Abdullakoya Haji v. Rubis Tharayil and other cases, to submit that the Respondent had failed to establish his financial capacity to pay the balance amount of consideration at the relevant time and had also failed to deposit the said amount in the court at the time of filing of the suit, he was not entitled to the discretionary relief of Specific Performance as granted by the Court, this court did not find any substance in any of the said submissions. As per the ratio of judgment laid down by the three-judge bench in case of Syed Dastagir, the compliance of readiness and willingness has to be in spirit and substance and not in letter and form, while making averments in the plaint. As per the Explanation (i) to Section 16(c), he need not tender to the Defendant or deposit the amount in the court, but he must aver performance of, or readiness and willingness to perform the contract according to its true construction. [21]

(ii) There was due compliance of Section 16(c) read with its Explanation on the part of the Respondent and that it was the Appellant who had failed to perform as per the terms of the agreement, though called upon by the Respondent to perform. The High Court also had rightly held that the Plaintiff had complied withs the requirements of Section 16(c) of the said Act by making a specific pleading with regard to his readiness and willingness and also proving the same by reliable evidence. This Court did not find any illegality or infirmity in the impugned judgment passed by the High Court. Therefore confirm the same, so far as granting of decree for specific performance of the agreement in question was concerned. [22]

Disposition: Appeal Dismissed

• • •

Katta Sujatha Reddy and Ors. vs. Siddamsetty Infra Projects Pvt. Ltd. and Ors. (25.08.2022 – SC) : MANU/SC/1046/2022

Relative Section:

Arbitration And Conciliation Act, 1996 - Section 9; Indian Contract Act, 1872 - Section 55; Specific Relief Act 1963 - Section 10, Specific Relief Act 1963 - Section 11(2), Specific Relief Act 1963 - Section 12, Specific Relief Act 1963 - Section 12(1), Specific Relief Act 1963 - Section 12(2), Specific Relief Act 1963 - Section 12(3), Specific Relief Act 1963 - Section 14, Specific Relief Act 1963 - Section 14(1), Specific Relief Act 1963 - Section 16, Specific Relief Act 1963 - Section 16(b), Specific Relief Act 1963 - Section 16(c), Specific Relief Act 1963 - Section 36, Specific Relief Act 1963 - Section 38, Specific Relief Act 1963 - Section 39, Specific Relief Act 1963 - Section 40, Specific Relief Act 1963 - Section 41, Specific Relief Act 1963 - Section 42; Specific Relief (Amendment) Act, 2018 - Section 3

Hon'ble Judges/Coram: N.V. Ramana, C.J.I., Krishna Murari and Hima Kohli, JJ.

Equivalent Citation:

AIR2022SC5435, 2022(6)ALD37, 2023(1)CivilCC(S.C.), 2022GLH(3)777, 2023(1)ICC543, 2022/INSC/863, (2022) 6MLJ630, 2023 (1) MWN 65, 2022(4)RCR(Civil)21, (2023)1SCC355

Number of Pages in the Original Judgment: 23

Case Reference:

Chand Rani (Dead) by Lrs. v. Kamal Rani (Dead) by Lrs. MANU/SC/ 0285/1993; Radheshyam Kamila v. Kiran Bala Dasi and Ors. MANU/WB/ 0072/1971; Adhunik Steels Ltd. v. Orissa Manganese and Minerals Pvt. Ltd. MANU/SC/2936/2007; Shyam Sunder and Ors. v. Ram Kumar and Ors. MANU/SC/0405/2001; Shanti Devi and Ors. v. Hukum Chand MANU/SC/ 0971/1996; Saradamani Kandappan and Ors. v. S. Rajalakshmi and Ors. MANU/SC/0717/2011; K.S. Vidyanadam and Ors. v. Vairavan MANU/SC/ 0404/1997; Jaswinder Kaur (now deceased) through her L.Rs. and Ors. v. Gurmeet Singh and Ors. MANU/SC/0550/2017; Abdul Rahim and Ors. v. Tufan Gazi and Ors. MANU/WB/0083/1928; William Graham v. Krishna

Chandra Dey MANU/PR/0011/1924; Rachakonda Narayana v. Ponthala Parvathamma and Ors. MANU/SC/0477/2001; Whiteley Limited v. Hilt (1918) 2 K.B. 808

Case Note:

Civil - Relief of specific performance - Section 12 of the Specific Relief Act, 1963 and Article 54 of the Limitation Act, 1963 - Present civil appeal arises out of the impugned judgment passed by the High Court granting relief to the purchaser - Whether the suit for specific performance is barred by limitation - Whether the amended Section 10 of the Specific Relief Act is prospective or retrospective in operation - Whether the purchaser is entitled to the relief of specific performance - In any case, whether the purchaser is entitled to take benefit of Section 12 of the Specific Relief Act in view of the part payment made in respect of the contract?

Facts:

A suit was filed for specific performance against the Appellants. It is argued that, Purchaser did not approach the Court with clean hands. The balance amount was not paid within the stipulated time period and the trial Court found the purchaser's statement regarding possession to be false. The suit filed by the purchaser is barred by limitation and the trial Court held so correctly. The parties executed the agreements to sell on 26.03.1997 and 27.03.1997 and the purchaser was to pay the balance amount within 3 months, i.e., by 27.06.1997. It is the purchaser's case that the vendors evaded execution of the sale deed as early as in June 1997. Therefore, the limitation would start running in June 1997 and expire in June 2000. The suit, however, was filed only on 09.08.2002 and is, therefore, clearly barred by limitation. The purchaser's oral evidence also shows that the right to sue accrued in the year 1997 itself. Additionally, the notice purportedly dated 08.02.2000, was actually despatched on 31.03.2000 and was purposely backdated. The purchaser was not ready and willing to perform the contract. The evidence on record indicates that the purchaser not only failed to pay the balance consideration within the stipulated 3 months, but also failed to pay the same within a period of 3 years of the agreement. A suit for specific performance cannot be decreed in a piecemeal manner. The High Court ought to have accepted the trial Court's decision and rejected the purchaser's appeal. Moreover, grant of specific relief only to the extent of 90% itself indicates that the purchaser was not ready and willing to perform the contract and consequently, is not entitled to the decree. The High Court, while overturning the trial Court's judgment, stated that the discretion to grant specific performance was taken away by the 2018 amendment to Section 10 of the Specific Relief Act. The impugned judgment erroneously states that the amendment is merely procedural and would apply retrospectively. The High Court has misconstrued Section 12 of the Specific Relief Act. The Section would not be applicable to the present case as the question of 'inability to perform a contract' does not arise.

Held, while allowing the appeal

1. Article 54 of the Limitation Act provides for two consequences based on the presence of fixed time period of performance. It is only in a case where the time period for performance is not fixed that the purchaser can take recourse to the notices issued and the vendors' reply thereto. In the case at hand, the aforesaid circumstances do not come into play as a fixed time period was clearly mandated by Clause 3 read with Clause 23 of the agreements to sell. [37]

2. The suit filed by the purchaser was clearly barred by limitation in view of the first part of Article 54 of the Limitation Act and no amount of payment of advance could have remedied such a breach of condition. [38]

3. When a substantive law is brought about by amendment, there is no assumption that the same ought to be given retrospective effect. Rather, there is a requirement for the legislature to expressly clarify whether the aforesaid amendments ought to be retrospective or not. [53]

4. Ordinarily, the effect of amendment by substitution would be that the earlier provisions would be repealed, and amended provisions would be enacted in place of the earlier provisions from the date of inception of that enactment. However, if the substituted provisions contain any substantive provisions which create new rights, obligations, or take away any vested rights, then such substitution cannot automatically be assumed to have come into force retrospectively. In such cases, the legislature has to expressly provide as to whether such substitution is to be construed retrospectively or not. [54]

5. In the case at hand, the amendment act contemplates that the said substituted provisions would come into force on such date as the Central Government may appoint, by notification in the Official Gazette, or different dates may be appointed for different provisions of the Act. It may be noted that 01.10.2018 was the appointed date on which the amended provisions would come into effect. [55]

6. The 2018 amendment to the Specific Relief Act is prospective and cannot apply to those transactions that took place prior to its coming into force. [56]

7. The purchaser did not voluntarily adhere to the time stipulation under the contract. In order to by-pass the condition of time being the essence, the purchaser invoked the standard of good faith. Aforesaid standard prescribes a higher duty of care for parties entering into a contract. Unless such duty is expressly stipulated, good faith standard cannot be implicitly read into any contract. [65]

8. Section 16(c) of the Specific Relief Act would only come into force if the purchaser was ready and willing to perform the contract within the three month period prescribed under Clause 3 of the agreements. The aforesaid conclusion is also bolstered by the fact that specific performance can only be granted when essential terms of contract are not violated in terms of Section 16(b). [68]

9. The purchaser was not ready or willing to perform his part of the contract within the time stipulated and accordingly, specific performance cannot be granted for the entire contract. [69]

10. The last aspect which has been argued concerns application of Section 12 of the Specific Relief Act, 1963. This issue arises from the fact that the purchaser is said to have paid 90 percent of the sale consideration and in lieu thereof, the High Court has held that the purchaser is entitled to ninety percent of the scheduled land. [74]

11. There was no inability on part of the parties to perform the rest of the contract or the remaining part was waived. In this case, the purchaser breached the essential condition of the contract, which altogether disentitles him to claim specific performance. There is no doubt that the claim of purchaser is hit by delay and laches on their part as they did not take appropriate measures within the stipulated time and filing of the suit was delayed by almost five years. [77]

12. Present Court do not think that it is an appropriate case for granting relief to the purchaser in terms of Section 12 of the Specific Relief Act, 1963 as the claim of the purchaser is barred by delay, laches and limitation. [78]

13. The contract was breached due to the conduct of the Plaintiff/ purchaser, who were not willing to perform the contract after entering into a time sensitive agreement. In any case, it is an admitted fact that Plaintiff had paid only part consideration. Though there is a forfeiture Clause in the agreement, this Court with a view of rendering complete justice between

the parties, deems it appropriate to direct the vendors/Appellants to repay the said amount with interest @ 7.5% p.a. from the date such payment was made by the purchaser to the vendors, till the entire amount is paid back. The vendors are directed to pay the entire amount to the credit of the suit account within six months from the date of receipt of a copy of the order. [79]

14. Appeal allowed. [80]
Disposition: Disposed of

• • •

PTC India Financial Services Limited vs. Venkateswarlu Kari and Ors. (12.05.2022 – SC) : MANU/SC/0629/2022

Relative Section:

Companies Act, 1956 - Section 150, Section 151, Section 152; Companies Act, 2013;

Consumer Protection Act, 1986; Depositories Act, 1996 - Section 2(1), Section 7, Section 10, Section 10(1), Section 11,Section 12,Section 12(1), Section 12(2), Section 25, Section 25(2),Section 28,Section 38(1);

Indian Contract Act, 1872 - Section 1,Section 51, Section 63,Section 148,Section 149,Section 150, Section 151, Section 152, Section 153,Section 154,Section 155,Section 156,Section 157,Section 158,Section 159,Section 160,Section 161,Section 162,`Section 163,Section 164,Section 165,Section 166,Section 167,Section 168 , Section 169,Section 170, Section 171, Section 172,Section 173,Section 174,Section 175,Section 176,Section 177, Section 178, Section 179;

Insolvency And Bankruptcy Code, 2016 - Section 7, Section 10, Section 10(4), Section 18;

Sale Of Goods Act, 1930 - Section 27;

Securities and Exchange Board of India (Depositories and Participants) Regulations, 1996 - Regulation 38(1), Regulation 58, Regulation 58(2), Regulation 58(3), Regulation 58(4),Regulation 58(5),Regulation 58(6), Regulation 58(8), Regulation 58(9);

Securities and Exchange Board of India (Substantial Acquisition of Shares and Takeovers) Regulations, 1997 - Regulation 7, Regulation 11(1);

Securities And Exchange Board Of India Act, 1992 - Section 12(1A);

Securitisation And Reconstruction Of Financial Assets And Enforcement Of Security Interest Act, 2002 - Section 2(1);

Specific Relief (Amendment) Act, 2018; Specific Relief Act 1963 - Section 10, Section 11,Section 11(2), Section 14, Section 16,Section 20,Section 38,Section 38(2),Section 38(3);

Transfer Of Property Act, 1882 - Section 69(3), Section 106
Hon'ble Judges/Coram:

M.R. Shah and Sanjiv Khanna, JJ.

Equivalent Citation: 2022(3)CTC412, 2022/INSC/561, 2022 (2) MWN 547, 2022(3)RCR(Civil)107, (2022)9SCC704, [2022]172SCL723(SC)

Number of Pages in the Original Judgment: 40

Case Reference:

Md. Sultan and Ors. v. Firm of Rampratap Kannyalal MANU/AP/0090/1964; Sri Raja Kakarlapudi Venkata Sudarsana Sundara Narasayyamma Garu (died) and Ors. v. Andhra Bank Ltd., Vijayawada and Ors. MANU/AP/0167/1960; Lallan Prasad v. Rahmat Ali and Ors. MANU/SC/0070/1966; The Bank of Bihar v. The State of Bihar and Ors. MANU/SC/0007/1971; Maharashtra State Co-operative Bank Ltd. v. The Assistant Provident Fund Commissioner MANU/SC/1727/2009; Karnataka Pawn Brokers Assn. and Ors. v. State of Karnataka and Ors. MANU/SC/0674/1998; Standard Chartered Bank and Ors. v. The Custodian and Ors. MANU/SC/0280/2000; M.R. Dhawan v. Madan Mohan and Ors. MANU/DE/0055/1969; Balkrishan Gupta and Ors. v. Swadeshi Polytex Ltd. and Ors. MANU/SC/0024/1985; Bank of Maharashtra v. Racmann Auto (P) Ltd. MANU/DE/0039/1991; Hulas Kunwar v. Allahabad Bank Ltd. MANU/WB/0159/1958; Haridas Mundra v. National and Grindlays Bank Ltd. MANU/WB/0030/1963; Vimal Chandra Grover v. Bank of India MANU/SC/0316/2000; The Official Assignee v. Madholal Sindhu MANU/MH/0052/1946; Krishna Bahadur v. Purna Theatre and Ors. MANU/SC/0667/2004; Ramdeyal Prasad v. Sayed Hasan MANU/BH/0102/1943; Dhani Ram and Sons v. The Frontier Bank Ltd. and Ors. MANU/PH/0101/1962; Kannambra Nayar Veettil Valia Ammukutti Neithiar v. P.N. Krishna Pattar and Ors. MANU/TN/0016/1942; Firm Thakur Das Marakhan Lal v. Mathura Prasad and Ors. MANU/UP/0021/1958; Commissioner of Wealth Tax v. Mahadeo Jalan and Mahabir Prasad Jalan and Ors. MANU/SC/0305/1972; Bharat Hari Singhania and Ors. v. Commissioner of Wealth Tax (Central) and Ors. MANU/SC/0312/1994; Simla Banking and Industrial Co. Ltd. v. Pritams MANU/PH/0199/1960; The Morvi Mercantile Bank Ltd. and Ors. v. Union of India (UOI), through The General Manager, Central Railway, Bombay MANU/SC/0064/1965; Reserve Bank of India v. Peerless General Finance and Investment Co. Ltd. and Ors. MANU/SC/0073/1987; Vasudev Ramchandra Shelat v. Pranlal Jayanand Thakar and Ors. MANU/SC/0033/1974; Seth Motilal Hirabhai and Ors. v. Bai Mani; F. Nanak Chand Ramkishan Das of Hodel and Ors. v. Lal Chand and Ors.; Rani Leasing & Finance Ltd. v. Sanjay Khemani; Kunj Behari Lal v. The Bhargava

Commercial Bank, Jubbulpore MANU/UP/0047/1918 : AIR 1918 All 363 (2); Soho Square Syndicate Ltd. v. Poland & Co. 1940-1 Ch 638; The Co-Operative Hindusthan Bank, Ltd. v. Surendranath De; Park Street Properties Private Limited v. Dipak Kumar Singh and Anr. MANU/SC/0960/2016 : (2016) 9 SCC 268; Nabha Investment Pvt. Ltd. v. Harmishan Dass Lukhmi Dass; Neikram Dobay v. Bank of Bengal, MANU/PR/0015/1891 : ILR (1892) 19 Cal 322; S.L. Ramaswamy Chetty and Anr. v. M.S.A.P.L. Palaniappa Chettiar; JRY Investments Private Limited v. Deccan Leafine Services Ltd. and Ors. MANU/MH/1427/2003 : (2004) 121 Comp Cas 12; Pushpanjali Tie Up Pvt. Ltd. v. Renudevi Choudhary and Ors.; Donald v. Suckling (1866) L.R. 1 Q.B. 585; Tendril Financial Services Pvt. Ltd. and Ors. v. Namedi Leasing & Finance Ltd. and Ors.; GTL Limited v. IFCI Ltd. and Ors.; Liquid Holdings Private Limited v. The Securities Exchange Board of India; Arjun Prasad and Ors. v. Central Bank of India Ltd.; Wilson v. Mcintosh 1894 A.C. P. 129; Corporation of the City of Tornoto v. John Russel; D. Jones & Smiths Reports 1908 Ac. 493; Selwyn v. Grafit 38 Ch. D.P. 273; Griffiths v. The Earl of Dudley 9, Q.B.D. P. 357; Vellayan Chettiar v. Government of the Province of Madras MANU/PR/0049/1947 : I.L.R. 1948 Mad. p. 214; Raja Chetty v. Jagannadhadas Govindas MANU/TN/0002/ 1946 : 1949 II M.L.J. P. 694

Case Note:

Contract - Pledge or hypothecation - Effect thereof on securities held in a depository - Section 176 of the Indian Contract Act, 1872 (Contract Act) - Depositories Act, 1996 read with the Regulation 58 of the Securities and Exchange Board of India (Depositories and Participants) Regulations, 1996 (1996 Regulations) - Whether the Depositories Act, 1996 read with the Regulation 58 of the 1996 Regulations has the legal effect of overwriting provisions relating to contracts of pledge under the Contract Act and common law as applicable in India?

Facts:

The primary legal issue that arose for consideration was whether the Depositories Act, 1996 read with the Regulation 58 of the 1996 Regulations has the legal effect of overwriting the provisions relating to the contracts of pledge under the Contract Act and the common law applicable in India. The issue arose from the claim raised by Appellant/ PIFSL, a wholly-owned subsidiary of PTC India Limited and registered with the Reserve Bank of India/ RBI as a Non-Banking Finance Company/ NBFC and classified as an Infrastructure Finance Company/ IFC. R2 had executed a Pledge Deed in favour of PIFSLpledging certain shares.Corporate Debtor filed a petition initiating corporate insolvency resolution process. R1 was appointed as Interim Resolution Professional/ IRP. PIFSL issued notice stating defaults on the part of Corporate Debtor. Debt since remained unpaid, PIFSL wrote to the Depository Participant invoking its rights in terms of the Pledge Deed. Acting on the request, the Depository Participant accorded PIFSL the status of 'beneficial owner' of pledged shares.PIFSL filed application as a financial creditor. Adjudicating Authority allowed PIFSL to withdraw the application with liberty to file proof of financial claim.Contrarily, PIFSL submitted Form C with a financial claim being the amount due and payable to PIFSL by the Corporate Debtor. IRPinformed that claim could not be crystalized as it was not possible to ascertain the value of shares 'transferred' to PIFSL. Similarly, PIFSL's claim cannot be crystalized due to the settlement in whole/part of its claim and the need to arrive at the valuation at the time of 'transfer' of shares to PIFSL.PIFSL and MHPL preferred separate applications before the Adjudicatory Authority against the rejections of their claims.By a common order the Adjudicating Authority disposed of the applications filed by PIFSL and MHPL, accepting the MHPL's claim by primarily relying on the Depositories Act and Regulation 58 of the 1996 Regulations. PIFSL challenged the orders before the National Company Law Appellate Tribunal but the appeals were dismissed vide the impugned judgment. Hence the present appeal.

Held, while allowing the Appeal:

Where money is advanced by way of the loan upon the security of goods, the transaction may take the form of a mortgage or pledge. The difference between a pledge and a mortgage of movable property is that while under a pledge there is only a bailment, whereas under a mortgage there is transfer of the right of the property by way of security. [4.3]

The pawnee has a conditional general property interest in the pledge, subject to the condition that he can pass on that general property if the pledge is brought to sale in accordance with the law.[5.4]

Any accretion in the shape of dividends, bonuses or right shares issued in respect of the pledged shares, in the absence of any contract to the contrary, is the special property of the pawnee as a security for the debt.[6.2]

Section 176 of the Contract Act requires that the pawnee may sell the thing pledged on giving the pawnor reasonable notice of the sale. It does not prescribe any fixed form of notice or specify any fixed period of notice. The object and purpose of giving notice is to make the pawnor know about the pawnee's intent to sell the pawn and give him an opportunity to exercise his statutory right of redemption, which as per Section 177 can be exercised till the date of 'actual sale'. Whether or not a notice was given and the period of notice was reasonable would depend upon the facts of the case. In view of the above discussion, the pawnor can communicate his willingness and desire to the pawnee that the pledged goods may be sold. In case any such request is made, a pawnee may well act upon the request without violating Section 176 of the Contract Act. However, a pawnee, unless he also agrees, cannot be compelled by the pawnor to sell the pledged goods.[7.3]

The Depositories Act is enacted to lay down a process and Rules for the dematerialization of securities by converting them into electronic data stored in the computers of 'the depository'.39 The Depositories Act establishes the depository eco-system and introduces the concepts of a 'registered owner'40 and 'beneficial owner'.41 Every owner of a physical share has to enter into an agreement with 'the depository' for availing its services. The physical certificate of security is cancelled. All securities held by 'the depository' are in a fungible form. 'The depository' becomes the 'registered owner' in respect of the security, whereas the person who surrenders the physical shares is recorded as 'the beneficial owner'. 'The depository', as the registered owner, does not have any voting right or any other right in respect of the securities held by it. 'The beneficial owner' shall be solely entitled to all rights, benefits, and liabilities attached to the securities held by 'the depository'. In terms of Section 11, every depository is mandated to maintain a register and index of 'beneficial owners' in the manner provided in Sections 150, 151 and 152 of the Companies Act, 1956. As per Section 742 of the Depositories Act, every 'depository', on receipt of intimation from a participant, is required to transfer the security in the transferee's name. Further, on registration of transfer of security in the transferee's name, the transferee is registered as the 'beneficial owner'.[9.3]

Power and right to transfer ownership of a dematerialised security vests with the 'beneficial owner', same as in the case of buying and selling physical securities. The difference lies in the delivery process in case of sale, and receipt in case of purchase, which is affected by the depository on instructions from the participant. Every person recorded as the 'beneficial owner' to transact and deal in securities must act through a participant who is an agent of the depository. Section 1043 states that notwithstanding any other law for the time being in force, 'the depository' shall be deemed as the 'registered owner' and is entitled to affect the transfer of ownership of the security on behalf of 'the beneficial owner'. No person, including the pawnee, can transfer the pawn held in dematerialised form without being registered as a 'beneficial owner'.[9.3]

It is absolutely necessary that the pawnee must be accorded status of 'beneficial owner' to enable him to exercise his right to sell the pledged dematerialized securities. The object is to ensure compliance with the procedure prescribed for the sale of dematerialised securities and not to interfere with the freedom to contract as long as they comply with the Contract Act and other laws. Further, if the terms of the pledge document violate Regulation 58(8), the pledge is not rendered void or illegal, albeit enforcement of the pledge viz. the dematerialised securities will be rendered unattainable unless steps are taken to act in accordance with the procedure prescribed by the 1996 Regulations.The pawnee would be entitled to sue the pawnor for recovery of money, breach of contract and may even apply for injunction/restrain on sale of dematerialised securities. However, third-party rights on transfer of the dematerialized securities, unless injuncted by a prior court order, would not be affected as long as the transfers are in terms of the Depositories Act and the 1996 Regulations.[9.4]

No derogation or conflict between Section 176 of the Contract Act and Sub-regulations (8) and (9) of Regulation 58. Regulation 58(8) entitles the pawnee to record himself as a 'beneficial owner' in place of the pawnor. This does not result in an 'actual sale'. The pawnee does not receive any money from such registration which he can adjust against the debt due. The pledge creates special rights including the right to sell the pawn to a third party and adjust the sale proceeds towards the debt in terms of Section 176 of the Contract Act. The reasoning that prior notice Under Section 176 of the Contract Act would interfere with transparency and certainty in the securities market and render fatal blow to the Depositories Act and the 1996 Regulations is farfetched as it fails to notice that the right of the pawnee is to realise money on sale of the security.[11.6]

Registration of the pawn, that is the dematerialised shares, in favour of PIFSL as the 'beneficial owner' does not have the effect of sale of shares by the pawnee. The pledge has not been discharged or satisfied either in full or in part. PIFSL is not required to account for any sale proceeds which are to be applied to the debt on the 'actual sale'. The two options available to PIFSL as the pawnee Under Section 176 of the Contract Act remain and are not exhausted.[12.7]

Appeal allowed and the impugned order passed by the Appellate Authority upholding the orders of the Adjudicating Authority and the emails of the IRP set aside.[13.1]

Disposition: Appeal Allowed

• • •

Veena Singh (Dead) through L.R. vs. The District Registrar / Additional Collector (F/R) and Ors. (10.05.2022 – SC) : MANU/SC/0615/2022

Relative Section:

Bihar Buildings (Lease, Rent and Eviction) Control Act, 1982;

Code of Civil Procedure, 1908 (CPC) - Section 9;

Constitution of India - Article 226;

Indian Contract Act, 1872;

Indian Evidence Act, 1872 - Section 68;

Indian Penal Code, 1860 (IPC) - Section 420, Section 467, Section 468, Section 471, Section 506; Indian Stamp Act, 1899 - Section 2(12);

Information Technology Act, 2000 - Section 11;

Madhya Pradesh Cooperative Societies Act, 1960;

Registration Act, 1908 - Section 17, Section 19, Section 20, Section 21, Section 23, Section 24, Section 25, Section 26, Section 32, Section 34,Section 34(1), Section 35, Section 35(1), Section 35(2), Section 35(3), Section 41, Section 43, Section 45, Section 58, Section 58(2), Section 59, Section 60, Section 61,Section 69, Section 71, Section 72, Section 72(1), Section 73, Section 73(1), Section 74, Section 74(a), Section 75, Section 75(1), Section 75(2), Section 75(3), Section 75(4), Section 76, Section 77, Section 88, Section 89;

Specific Relief Act 1963 - Section 31(2);

Transfer Of Property Act, 1882 - Section 107

Hon'ble Judges/Coram:

Dr. D.Y. Chandrachud, A.S. Bopanna and Bela M. Trivedi, JJ

Equivalent Citation:

2022(7)ADJ49, 2022(5)BLJ18, 2022 (3) CCC 187 , 2022/INSC/543, 2022(3)RCR(Civil)6, (2022)7SCC1, [2022]3SCR736

Number of Pages in the Original Judgment:34

Case Reference:

Satya Pal Anand v. State of M.P. and Ors. MANU/SC/1359/2016; Rajendra Pratap Singh v. Rameshwar Prasad MANU/SC/0669/1998; Suraj Lamp and Industries (P) Ltd. thru. DIR v. State of Haryana and Ors. MANU/

SC/1021/2009; Jambu Parshad v. Muhammad Aftab Ali Khan and Anr. MANU/PR/0019/1914; Government of Uttar Pradesh and Ors. v. Raja Mohammad Amir Ahmad Khan MANU/SC/0030/1961; N.M. Ramachandraiah v. State of Karnataka; Banasettappa Laljichikkanna v. District Registrar; Sayyapparaju Surayya v. Ramchandar Prasad Singh and Ors.; Jogesh Prasad Singh and Ors. v. Ramchandar Prasad Singh and Ors.; Ebadut Ali v. Muhammad Fareed MANU/BH/0129/1916 : AIR (3) 1916 Pat 206 : 35 Ind. Cas. 56; Ghasita Ram Bajaj v. Raj Kamal Radio Electronic; Kamlabai v. Shantirai; S. Ramamurthy v. Jayalakshmi Ammal; Union Bank of India v. Dhian Pati; Bank of Baroda v. Shree Moti Industries; Bharat Indu and Ors. v. Hakim Mohammad Hamid Ali Khan; Smt. Raisa Begam v. District Registrar, Saharanpur and Anr.; Mohima Chunder Dhur v. Jugul Kishore Bhutta Charji, MANU/WB/0181/1881 : ILR Volume VII Calcutta; Smt. Uma Devi v. Narayan Nayak; Bhutkani Nath v. Smt. Kamaleswari Nath MANU/GH/0087/1971 : AIR 1972 Assam and Nagaland 15; Puran Chand Nahatta v. Monmotho Nath Mukherji and Ors.

Case Note:

Civil - Registration of Sale deed - Forgery alleged - Section 72 of the Indian Registration Act, 1908 - Appellant sought Sub-Registrar to take requisite action against R2 - Registration of sale deed accordingly refused - Appeal filed allowed and sale deed was registered - In the meantime Appellant got FIR also registered - Appellant further challenged order by way of writ - Petition was dismissed while leaving it open to Appellant to move civil court for a declaration that sale deed was obtained by fraud and thus a nullity - Hence the present appeal - Whether the recourse by the second Respondent against the order of the Sub-Registrar would deprive them of any remedy whatsoever? - Whether Appellant's admission of her signatures and thumb impressions/fingerprints on the sale deed amounted to an admission of "execution"?

Facts:

In the instant case, sale deed in question was sought to be refused registration on Appellant's alleged claim that it was obtained by fraud and thus a nullity. The Sub-Registrar declined to register the sale deed. However in appeal preferred, execution was found to be valid and accordingly it was directed to be registered. Appellant also got an FIR registered in the meantime. Besides, Appellant challenged the order of the District Registrar by filing writ. In adjudicating the Appellant's writ petition by the impugned judgment Ld. Single Judge observed that the writ petition was instituted after the registration of the FIR by the Appellant, prior to which the order of the District Registrar had already been complied with by the registration of the sale deed. The Single Judge noted Appellant making improvement also in the statements. It was held that writ court does not have the jurisdiction to decide on the issue and gave liberty to raise claim before the civil court. Hence the present appeal.

Held, while allowing the Appeal:

In the event of a refusal by the Registrar, a suit can be filed by a party in terms of the provisions of Section 7712 before a civil court, praying for a decree directing the document to be registered. On the other hand, an order of the Registrar directing the registration of a document is amenable to a challenge Under Article 226 of the Constitution. While seeking a writ of certiorari, the person moving the petition before the High Court would be entitled to establish whether the registration has been ordered in breach of the statutory provisions and is contrary to law. The mere existence of the remedy available before a civil court, under Section 9 of the Code of Civil Procedure to avoid the document or to seek a declaration in regard to its invalidity, will not divest a person, who complains that the order passed by Registrar for the registration of the document was contrary to statutory provisions, of the remedy which is available in the exercise of a court's writ jurisdiction under Article 226 of the Constitution. Undoubtedly, whether a writ should be entertained lies at the discretion of the court and in a given case, the High Court may decline to do so on the ground that disputed questions of fact arise. However, it needs to be emphasized that in the exercise of the writ jurisdiction, it would be open to the High Court to determine as to whether the statutory provisions which guide the power of the Sub-Registrar or, as the case may be, the Registrar to order the registration of the document have been duly fulfilled.[30]

In the present case, the appeal before the Registrar was not maintainable Under Section 72. Indeed, the Appellant, in response to the memo of appeal filed by the second Respondent, specifically pleaded in her objections that "hearing the appeal under Section 72 of the Indian Registration Act or to deliver any judgment will be against law". At the same time, however, the Appellant also pleaded that she "had full right for argument under Section 75(4) of the Indian Registration Act and under the Code of Civil Procedure, 1908 from the witnesses and the Appellant". The Registrar is empowered to summon witnesses under Section 75(4) for the purpose of an enquiry under Sections 73 and 74. It thus emerges that the parties proceeded on the basis that the proceedings would be decided on the basis of an enquiry under Section 73, and the enquiry was conducted with reference to the provisions of Section 74. The Appellant herself understood this to be the position in her objections filed to the appeal filed by the second Respondent, since she invoked her rights under Section 75(4), which applies to enquiry proceedings Under Section 74. The appeal against the Sub-Registrar's order was not maintainable under Section 72. The remedy of the second Respondent, where the Sub-Registrar refused registration on the ground that the Appellant denied execution of the document, was under Section 73. The Registrar conducted an enquiry under the provisions of Sections 73 and 74. Both parties participated in the enquiry.[36]

Thus, the mis-labelling of an application Under Section 73 as an appeal Under Section 72 would by itself not vitiate the proceedings before the Registrar. This becomes especially true when proceedings before the Registrar, in substance, were proceedings Under Section 73 itself and both the parties acknowledged them to be so, explicitly or by their conduct. Therefore, the second Respondent's mis-labelling of their application as an appeal Under Section 72 will not vitiate the proceedings which led to the District Registrar's order.[38]

The "execution" of a document does not stand admitted merely because a person admits to having signed the document. Such an interpretation accounts for circumstances where an individual signs a blank paper and it is later converted into a different document, or when an individual is made to sign a document without fully understanding its contents. Adopting a contrary interpretation would unfairly put the burden upon the person denying execution to challenge the registration before a civil court or a writ court, since registration will have to be allowed once the signature has been admitted.[57]

Therefore, in a situation where an individual admits their signature on a document but denies its execution, the Sub-Registrar is bound to refuse registration in accordance with Sections 35(3)(a) of the Registration Act. Subsequently, if an application if filed Under Section 73, the Registrar is entrusted with the power of conducting an enquiry of a quasi-judicial nature Under Section 74. If the Registrar passes an order refusing registration Under Section 76, the party presenting the document for registration has the remedy of filing a civil suit Under Section 77 of the Registration Act, where a competent civil court will be able to adjudicate upon the question of fact conclusively.[64]

The Registrar purported to exercise the powers conferred Under Section 74 and arrived at a finding that the sale deed had been duly signed by the Appellant and was therefore liable to be registered. However, the objections of the Appellant raised serious issues of a triable nature which could only have been addressed before and adjudicated upon by a court of competent civil jurisdiction. Registrar in the present case acted contrary to law by directing the sale deed to be registered.[68]

The Single Judge of the High Court has, with respect, conflated the mere signing of the sale deed with its execution. Such an approach is completely erroneous and cannot be upheld.[69]

Appeal accordingly allowed and the impugned judgment set aside. [70]

Disposition: Appeal Allowed

• • •

Leeladhar (D) thr. L.Rs. vs. Vijay Kumar (D) thr. L.Rs. and Ors. (26.09.2019 – SC) : MANU/SC/1330/2019

Relative Section: Specific Relief Act 1963 - Section 20(2)(c)

Hon'ble Judges/Coram: Deepak Gupta and Aniruddha Bose, JJ.

Equivalent Citation:

2020(212)AIC245, AIR2019SC4652, 2019(6)ALD39, 2020 (141) ALR 718, 2019(6)ALT89, 2019(6)BLJ84, 2019(1) CivilCC (S.C.), 2019(4) Civil CC (S.C.), 2019(II)CLR(SC)1239, 2019/INSC/1085, 2019(4)RCR (Civil) 685, 2020 149 RD290, 2019(13)SCALE81, (2020)19SCC336

Number of Pages in the Original Judgment: 4

Case Reference: nil

Case Note:

Property - Specific performance - Section 20 of the Specific Relief Act, 1963 - Challenge in present case was relating to decree of specific performance granted in favour of Plaintiffs-Respondents - Whether decree of specific performance could not have been granted in favour of Plaintiffs-Respondents.

Facts:

One Leeladhar, the original Appellant herein, entered into an agreement to sell 18 bighas of land for a sum of Rs. 40,000 with Deshraj, father of the Plaintiffs-Respondents herein on 15.02.1985. Admittedly, an amount of Rs. 35,000 was paid in advance. This agreement to sell was registered on 18.02.1985. On 26.03.1985 another document (Exhibit P-14) was entered into between the parties. Leeladhar was paid balance Rs. 5,000/- and the subsequent agreement notes that he gave possession of the land to Deshraj. On 20.01.1988, Deshraj issued a legal notice to Leeladhar asking him to get the sale deed executed. According to the Plaintiffs, they and their father went to the office of the Sub-Registrar on 15.02.1988 for this purpose. But Leeladhar did not turn up. Deshraj expired on 16.05.1988 and, thereafter, the Respondents herein filed a suit in the Court of Civil Judge, Nainital praying for specific performance of the contract and also prayed that if any part of the disputed land is not found in their possession, then possession be given to them. In the alternative, they prayed for refund of Rs. 40,000 along with interest. In the written statement, Leeladhar took the plea that the agreement in question was a sham document. Deshraj was a moneylender but did not have a licence to do money lending. Therefore, he used to get such documents executed to secure the loans advanced by him. It was also pleaded that Leeladhar had returned the entire amount along with interest to Deshraj on 03.03.1987. This suit was decreed by the trial court. Leeladhar filed an appeal, which was partly allowed by the first appellate court holding that the Plaintiffs were not entitled to the discretionary relief of specific performance. This judgment was challenged before the High Court. The second appeal was allowed and the matter was remanded to the first appellate court to decide the case afresh in light of the provisions of Section 20(2)(c) of Act, 1963. After remand, the Additional District Judge dismissed the appeal of Leeladhar and upheld the order of the trial court. The second appeal filed by Leeladhar before the High Court was dismissed and, hence, this appeal.

Held, while dismissing the appeal

1. The agreement to sell (Exhibit P-13) is registered on 18.02.1985. Rs. 35,000 out of Rs. 40,000 was paid. The balance Rs. 5,000 was paid when the document (Exhibit P-14) was executed on 26.03.1985. As far as delay is concerned, we are of the considered view that there is no delay in filing the suit. The suit is within limitation. Further, in this case, even as per the Appellants, the possession of the land was with the Plaintiffs-Respondents. Therefore, they were in no hurry to get the sale deed executed and this does not disentitle them from getting the relief of specific performance. [4]

2. As far as the issue of Deshraj being a moneylender and having got this document executed only to secure repayment of amount is concerned, all the courts below have found as a fact that this is not the case. The finding is that an agreement to sell was executed. After remand, the first appellate court clearly held that the documents in question relied upon by Leeladhar could not be used by him because they were only copies and if actually, he had repaid those loans then he would have got originals back from Deshraj. The agreement was an agreement to sell and after entering into the agreement to sell, Leeladhar received the full sale consideration and handed over the possession to Deshraj,the question of exercising any discretionary favour to the Appellant does not arise. [5]

3. To take benefit of Clause (c) of Sub-section (2) of Section 20 of the Specific Relief Act, the Defendant in a suit for specific performance

must show that he entered into the contract under the circumstances which though rendering the contract voidable, make it inequitable. In the present case, once it is held that the document entered was an agreement to sell and not a sham transaction, the Appellants can take no benefit of this provision. [7]

4. Appeal dismissed. [8]

• • •

CHAPTER VIII

Ferrodous Estates (Pvt.) Ltd. vs. P. Gopirathnam (Dead) and Ors. (12.10.2020 – SC) : MANU /SC /0750/2020

Relative Section:

Bihar Tenancy Act, 1885 - Section 26N, Section 26(O); Bihar Tenancy Amendment Act, 1934; Bombay Tenancy and Agricultural Lands Act, 1948; Code of Civil Procedure, 1908 (CPC); General Clauses Act 1897 - Section 6; Indian Contract Act, 1872 - Section 23; Motor Vehicles Act, 1939; Punjab Relief Of Indebtedness Act, 1934 - Section 5, Punjab Relief Of Indebtedness Act, 1934 - Section 6; Specific Relief (Amendment) Act, 2018; Specific Relief Act 1963 - Section 16(c), Specific Relief Act 1963 - Section 20, Specific Relief Act 1963 - Section 20(1), Specific Relief Act 1963 - Section 20(2); Tamil Nadu Urban Land (Ceiling & Regulation) Repeal Act, 1999; Tamil Nadu Urban Land (ceiling And Regulation) Act, 1978 - Section 4, Tamil Nadu Urban Land (ceiling And Regulation) Act, 1978 - Section 5, Tamil Nadu Urban Land (ceiling And Regulation) Act, 1978 - Section 5(3), Tamil Nadu Urban Land (ceiling And Regulation) Act, 1978 - Section 6, Tamil Nadu Urban Land (ceiling And Regulation) Act, 1978 - Section 7, Tamil Nadu Urban Land (ceiling And Regulation) Act, 1978 - Section 11, Tamil Nadu Urban Land (ceiling And Regulation) Act, 1978 - Section 11(1), Tamil Nadu Urban Land (cciling And Regulation) Act, 1978 - Section 11(3), Tamil Nadu Urban Land (ceiling And Regulation) Act, 1978 - Section 11(4), Tamil Nadu Urban Land (ceiling And Regulation) Act, 1978 - Section 17, Tamil Nadu Urban Land (ceiling And Regulation) Act, 1978 - Section 19, Tamil Nadu Urban Land (ceiling And Regulation) Act, 1978 - Section 21, Tamil Nadu Urban Land (ceiling And Regulation) Act, 1978 - Section 21(1), Tamil Nadu Urban Land (ceiling And Regulation) Act, 1978 - Section 23; Land Acquisition Act, 1894; Urban Land (ceiling And Regulation) Act, 1976 - Section 20; Usurious Loans Act, 1918 - Section 3

Hon'ble Judges/Coram:

Rohinton Fali Nariman and Navin Sinha, JJ.

Equivalent Citation:

AIR2020SC5041, 2021(1)ALD4, 2020(6)ALT19, 2021(2)BLJ97, 2020 (4) CCC 185 , 2021(1)CivilCC(S.C.), 2021(2)ICC298, 2020/INSC/586, 2021-1-LW388, [2020]13SCR673

Number of Pages in the Original Judgment: 36

Case Reference:

Jambu Rao Satappa Kocheri v. Neminath Appayya Hanammannaver MANU/SC/0178/1968; Union of India (UOI) and Ors. v. Valluri Basavaiah Chowdhary and Ors. MANU/SC/0539/1979; Shah Jitendra Nanalal v. Patel Lallubhai Ishverbhai MANU/GJ/0076/1984; Shoba Viswanatha v. D.P. Kingsley MANU/TN/0646/1996; Mathura Prasad Bajoo Jaiswal and Ors. v. Dossibai N.B. Jeejeebhoy MANU/SC/0420/1970; Sushila v. Nihalchand Nahata MANU/TN/1841/2003; Ram Kristo Mandal and Ors. v. Dhankisto Mandal MANU/SC/0369/1968; Vishwa Nath Sharma v. Shyam Shankar Goela and Ors. MANU/SC/7169/2007; Motilal and Ors. v. Nanhelal and Anr. MANU/PR/0061/1930; Chandnee Widya Vati Madden v. C.L. Katial and Ors. MANU/SC/0257/1963; R.C. Chandiok and Ors. v. Chuni Lal Sabharwal and Ors. MANU/SC/0033/1970; Bhim Singhji and Ors. v. Union of India (UOI) and Ors. MANU/SC/0509/1980; Durga Prasad and Ors. v. Deep Chand and Ors. MANU/SC/0008/1953; Motilal Jain v. Ramdasi Devi and Ors. MANU/SC/0438/2000; Nirmala Anand v. Advent Corporation Pvt. Ltd. and Ors. MANU/SC/0455/2002; HPA International and Ors. v. Bhagwandas Fateh Chand Daswani and Ors. MANU/SC/0536/2004; Aniglase Yohannan v. Ramlatha and Ors. MANU/SC/0653/2005; Van Vibhag Karamchari Griha Nirman Sahkari Sanstha Maryadit v. Ramesh Chander and Ors. MANU/SC/0866/2010; Immani Appa Rao and Ors. v. Gollapalli Ramalingamurthi and Ors. MANU/SC/0051/1961; Gajraj Singh and Ors. v. The State Transport Appellate Tribunal and Ors. MANU/SC/0116/1997; India Tobacco Co. Ltd. v. The Commercial Tax Officer, Bhavanipore and Ors. MANU/SC/0353/1974; Rameshwar and Ors. v. Jot Ram and Ors. MANU/SC/0512/1975; Pasupuleti Venkateswarlu v. The Motor & General Traders MANU/SC/0415/1975; Bhajan Lal v. State of Punjab and Ors. MANU/SC/0384/1970; Lachmeshwar Prasad Shukul and Ors. v. Keshwar Lal Chaudhuri and Ors. MANU/FE/0002/1940; Ramji Lal Ram Lal and Ors. v. State of Punjab and Ors. MANU/PH/0272/1965; Dayawati and Ors. v. Inderjit and Ors. MANU/SC/0022/1966; Amarjit Kaur v. Pritam Singh and Ors. MANU/SC/0006/1974; Lakshmi Narayan Guin and Ors. v. Niranjan Modak MANU/SC/0316/1984; Ram Sarup v. Munshi and Ors. MANU/SC/0401/1962; Mula and Ors. v. Godhu and Ors. MANU/

SC/0373/1969; Keshavan Madhava Menon v. The State of Bombay MANU/ SC/0020/1951; Nirmala Anand v. Advent Corporation (P) Ltd. and Ors. MANU/SC/0845/2002; P. D'Souza v. Shondrilo Naidu MANU/SC/0561/ 2004; P.S. Ranakrishna Reddy v. M.K. Bhagyalakshmi and Ors. MANU/SC/ 7148/2007; Jai Narain Parasrampuria (Dead) and Ors. v. Pushpa Devi Saraf and Ors. MANU/SC/8451/2006; Narinderjit Singh v. North Star Estate Promoters Ltd. MANU/SC/0417/2012; K. Narendra v. Riviera Apartments (P) Ltd. MANU/SC/0392/1999; Satya Jain (D) Thr. L.Rs. and Ors. v. Anis Ahmed Rushdie (D) Thr. L.Rs. and Ors. MANU/SC/1063/2012; K. Prakash v. B.R. Sampath Kumar MANU/SC/0850/2014; Zarina Siddiqui v. A. Ramalingam MANU/SC/0975/2014; Sunkara Lakshminarasamma (D) by L.Rs. v. Sagi Subba Raju and Ors. MANU/SC/1351/2018; Madamsetty Satyanarayana v. G. Yellogi Rao and Ors. MANU/SC/0310/1964; K.S. Vidyanadam and Ors. v. Vairavan MANU/SC/0404/1997; S.V. Sankaralinga Nadar v. P.T.S. Ratnaswami Nadar and Ors. MANU/TN/0191/1952; Jiwan Lal and Ors. v. Brij Mohan Mehra and Ors. MANU/SC/0015/1972; Chand Rani (Dead) by Lrs. v. Kamal Rani (Dead) by Lrs. MANU/SC/0285/1993; Saradamani Kandappan and Ors. v. S. Rajalakshmi and Ors. MANU/SC/ 0717/2011; Nanjappan v. Ramasamy and Ors. MANU/SC/0203/2015; Jacques v. Withy 1 H. Bl. 65; Hitchcock v. Way (1837) 6 A & E 943 : 112 ER 360; Narayanamma v. Govindappa; Patterson v. State of Alabama MANU/ USSC/0102/1935 : (1934) 294 US 600; Steward v. North Metropolitan Tramways Co. (1885) 16 QBD 178; Quilter v. Maple Son (1882) 9 QBD 672; Stovin v. Fairbrass (1919) 88 LJ KB 1004; Mukerjee (K.C.) v. Mst. Ramaraton MANU/PR/0060/1935 : 63 IA 47; Attorney-General v. Sillem 11 ER 1200; Kristnama Chariar v. Mangammal ILR (1902) 26 Mad 91 (FB); John Lemm v. Thomas Alexander Mitchell (1912) A.C. 400; Kay v. Goodwin MANU/INOT/0001/1830 : 130 E.R. 1403 (1830); Anis Ahmed Rushdie v. Bhiku Ram Jain RFA (OS) No. 11 of 1984; A. Ramalingam v. H. Siddiqui RFA No. 265 of 1999; Ramathal v. Maruthathal MANU/SC/1154/2017 : (2018) 18 SCC 303; Chokalingam Chetty Case 54 MLJ 88 (PC)

Case Note:

Civil - Suit for Specific Performance - Agreement to Sell - Vacant land (Suit Property)-Land in excess of ceiling limit - Embargo of Section 5(3) read with Section 6 of the Tamil Nadu Urban Land Ceiling Act, 1978 - Respondent failed to obtain due permissions from concerned authorities (land ceiling)- Suit decreed by Ld. Singh Judge with direction to Respondents toexecute sale deed- Appeal preferred before Division Bench which on several questions raised Reference - Thereafter case was remanded back to Ld. Single Judge and against came up in appeal - Division Bench vide impugned judgment set aside the findings of Ld. Single Judge - Hence, the present appeal - Whether Division Bench rightly applied the law laid in the background of facts and thereby holding Appellant not entitled to decree of Specific Performance?

Facts:

The present appeal is in reference to exercise of discretionary jurisdiction under Section 20 of the Specific Performance Act. In the present matter, an agreement to sell was executed between Appellant Company and Respondents. As per the agreement, Respondents were required to obtain due permission from land ceiling authorities pertaining to sale of vacant land. The Respondents failed to perform their part of obligations, however resisted claims of Appellant on the ground of short payment. Ld. Single Judge decreed the suit which however was reversed by the Division bench in appeal. The Division bench vide impugned judgment held Appellant as not entitled to decree of specific performance on the ground of claim being liable to hit by provisions of Sections 5(3) and 6 of the Tamil Nadu Urban Land Ceiling Act. Hence, the present appeal.

Held, while allowing the appeal:

i. A suit for specific performance filed within limitation cannot be dismissed on the sole ground of delay or laches. However, an exception to this Rule is where immovable property is to be sold within a certain period, time being of the essence, and it is found that owing to some default on the part of the Plaintiff, the sale could not take place within the stipulated time. Once a suit for specific performance has been filed, any delay as a result of the court process cannot be put against the Plaintiff as a matter of law in decreeing specific performance. However, it is within the discretion of the Court, regard being had to the facts of each case, as to whether some additional amount ought or ought not to be paid by the Plaintiff once a decree of specific performance is passed in its favour, even at the appellate stage. [31]

ii.The Defendants were held to have taken up dishonest pleas and also held to have been in breach of a solemn agreement in which they were to obtain the Urban Land Ceiling permission which, if not obtained, would, under the agreement itself, not stand in the way of the specific performance of the agreement between the parties. He who asks for equity must do equity. Given the conduct of the Defendants in this case, as contrasted with the conduct of the Appellant who is ready and willing throughout to perform its part of the bargain, present is a fit case in which the Division Bench judgment should be set aside. As a result, the decree passed by the Single Judge is restored. Since the Appellant itself offered a sum of Rs. 1.25 crores to the Division Bench, it must be made to pay this amount to the Respondents within a period of eight weeks from the date of this judgment. [32]

iii. Appeal allowed [33]

• • •

Deccan Paper Mills Co. Ltd. vs. Regency Mahavir Properties and Ors. (19.08.2020 – SC) : MANU/SC/0599/2020

Relative Section:

Indian Partnership Act, 1932; Andhra Pradesh Land Reforms (Ceiling on Agricultural Holdings) Act, 1973; Arbitration Act, 1940 - Section 20; Arbitration and Conciliation (Amendment) Act, 2015; Arbitration And Conciliation Act, 1996 - Section 8, Arbitration And Conciliation Act, 1996 - Section 16; Companies Act, 1956; Court-fees Act, 1870 - Section 7(iv); Indian Contract Act, 1872 - Section 11, Indian Contract Act, 1872 - Section 17; Indian Evidence Act, 1872 - Section 65(e), Indian Evidence Act, 1872 - Section 74, Indian Evidence Act, 1872 - Section 74(2); Land Acquisition Act, 1898; Maharashtra Court-fees Act - Section 6(4); Registration Act, 1908 - Section 61(2);

Specific Relief Act 1963 - Section 4, Section 10, Section 20, Section 26(1), Section 26(3),Section 27,Section 27(1),Section 27(2), Section 29, Section 30,Section 31,Section 31(1), Section 31(2), Section 32, Section 33, Section 33(1), Section 34, Section 34(2), Section 35;

Specific Relief Act, 1877 - Section 35, Specific Relief Act, 1877 - Section 39, Specific Relief Act, 1877 - Section 39(1), Specific Relief Act, 1877 - Section 41, Specific Relief Act, 1877 - Section 42, Specific Relief Act, 1877 - Section 43; Transfer of Property Act, 1882

Hon'ble Judges/Coram:

Rohinton Fali Nariman, Navin Sinha and Indira Banerjee, JJ.

Equivalent Citation: 2020(216)AIC49, AIR2020SC4047, 2020(6)ALD71, 2020(6)ALLMR614, 2021 (144) ALR 250, 2020(4)ARBLR468(SC), 2021 2 AWC1819SC, 2020(5)BLJ471, 2020(5)BomCR368, 2021(4)CTC334, 2020(II)CLR(SC)869, 2020/INSC/497, 2020(5)KLT108, 2021(4)MhLj692, (2020)6MLJ524, 2021 150 RD709, (2021)4SCC786, 2020 (7-8) SCJ 9, [2020]13SCR427

Number of Pages in the Original Judgment: 23

Case Reference:

Swiss Timing Limited v. Organising Committee, Commonwealth Games 2010 MANU/ SC/ 0516/2014; N. Radhakrishnan v. Maestro Engineers and Ors. MANU/SC/1758/2009; S.B.P. and Co. v. Patel Engineering Ltd. and Ors. MANU/SC/1787/2005; Booz Allen and Hamilton Inc. v. SBI Home Finance Ltd. and Ors. MANU/SC/0533/2011; Aliens Developers Private Limited v. M. Janardhan Reddy and Ors. MANU/AP/0525/2015; Rashid Raza v. Sadaf Akhtar MANU/SC/1249/2019; The State of Andhra Pradesh and Ors. v. T. Suryachandra Rao MANU/SC/0431/2005; Ameet Lalchand Shah and Ors. v. Rishabh Enterprises and Ors. MANU/SC/0501/2018; Mayavti Trading Pvt. Ltd. v. Pradyuat Deb Burman MANU/SC /1232/2019; Emaar MGF Land Limited v. Aftab Singh MANU/SC/1458/2018; Olympus Superstructures Pvt. Ltd. v. Meena Vijay Khetan and Ors. MANU/SC/0359/ 1999; Sulochana Uppal v. Surinder Sheel Bhakri MANU/DE/0560/1990; Shravan Goba Mahajan v. Kashiram Devji MANU/MH/0139/1926; Muppudathi Pillai v. Krishnaswami Pillai and Ors. MANU/TN/0455/1959; Md. Noorul Hoda v. Bibi Raifunnisa and Ors. MANU/SC/1414/1996; Gopal Das and Anr. v. Sri Thakurji and Ors. MANU/PR/0002/1943; Smt. Rekha Rana and Ors. v. Smt. Ratnashree Jain MANU/MP/0544/2005; R. Viswanathan v. Rukn-Ul-Mulk Syed Abdul Wajid MANU/SC/0038/1962; Satrucharla Vijaya Rama Raju v. Nimmaka Jaya Raju and Ors. MANU/SC/ 2505/2005; Razia Begum v. Sahebzadi Anwar Begum and Ors. MANU/SC/ 0003/1958; Suhrid Singh v. Randhir Singh and Ors. MANU/SC/0210/2010; M/s. P.N. B. Finance Ltd. v. Shital Prasad Jain and others MANU/DE/0002/ 1991; Yanala Malleshwari and Ors. v. Ananthula Sayamma and Ors. MANU/ AP/0747/2006; Avitel Post Studioz Limited and Ors. v. HSBC PI Holding (Mauritius) Ltd. Appeal No. 196 of 2014 and Civil Appeal No. 5145 of 2016; Satish Sood v. Gujarat Tele Links Pvt. Ltd. 2014 (1) AIR Bom R 27

Case Note:

Arbitration - Arbitrability of Dispute - Serious Fraud alleged - Jurisdiction of Arbitrator - Appellant contended that when it comes to serious allegations of fraud, an arbitrator's jurisdiction gets ousted - It was further contended that both the Courts below did not look into the requirements of the amended Section 8 of the Arbitration and Conciliation Act, 1996 while referring parties to Arbitration - Hence, the present Appeal - Whether the matter was rightly referred to arbitration?

Facts:

Appellant and R2 had executed an Agreement (dated 22.07.2004) for developing a portion of land. This agreement had a clause whereby owner was stated to have no objection if at any stage during the continuance of this agreement the Developer assigns, delegates the rights, under this agreement or the Power of Attorney/writings executed in furtherance hereof to any other person, firm or party without violating or disturbing any of the terms and conditions of this agreement. There was no arbitration clause in the agreement. Subsequently, R2 and R1, a partnership firm executed an agreement whereby R2 assigned the execution of the agreement dated 22.07.2004 to R3 and this agreement contained an arbitration clause. A deed of confirmation followed, by which it was stated that this deed was to be treated as part of the 20.05.2006 agreement, in which the assignment by R2 to R1 was reaffirmed. Appellant alleged fraud being played by R3 on the ground of making representations for diverse reasons as he intended to develop the property in question through a partnership firm by other name and had further assured himself as to be one of the leading partners of the said firm. There were other allegations also levelled eventually leading to serious fraud being allegedly committed. All the agreements as executed, including the confirmation deed were accordingly sought to be declared a nullity and thus cancellation thereof and not binding upon the Appellant. Sometime later an application was filed for invoking arbitration clause as per one of the agreement between R2 and R1 and it was held by the lower Court that when there is a Clause of arbitration it is mandated on the Civil Court to refer the dispute and parties for arbitration as per agreement. It was held that the Appellants have materially contented about playing fraud by R3 but there was no such content in agreement as alleged by Appellant in plaint about keeping faith on R3. Application was allowed and Appellant was directed to get the alleged dispute resolved through the process of arbitration. Appellant filed a writ petition which was disposed of by the impugned judgment in which it was held that following the judgment of the Single Judge in Swiss Timing Ltd. v. Commonwealth Games 2010 Organising Committee, that the decision in N. Radhakrishnan v. Maestro Engineers, it would not be possible to follow the same, as a result of which the "fraud exception" was rejected. The writ petition was accordingly dismissed, with the result that the parties stood referred to arbitration. Hence, the present Appeal.

Held, while dismissing the Appeals:

When Sections 34 and 35 are seen, the position becomes even clearer. Unlike Section 31, under Section 34, any person entitled to any legal character may institute a suit for a declaration that he is so entitled.

Considering that it is possible to argue on a reading of this provision that the legal character so declared may be against the entire world, Section 35 follows, making it clear that such declaration is binding only on the parties to the suit and persons claiming through them, respectively. This is for the reason that Under Section 4 of the Specific Relief Act, specific relief is granted only for the purpose of enforcing individual civil rights. The principle contained in Section 4 permeates the entire Act, and it would be most incongruous to say that every other provision of the Specific Relief Act refers to in personam actions, Section 31 alone being out of step, i.e., referring to in rem actions. [22]

When it comes to cancellation of a deed by an executant to the document, such person can approach the Court Under Section 31, but when it comes to cancellation of a deed by a non-executant, the non-executant must approach the Court Under Section 34 of the Specific Relief Act, 1963. Cancellation of the very same deed, therefore, by a non-executant would be an action in personam since a suit has to be filed Under Section 34. However, cancellation of the same deed by an executant of the deed, being Under Section 31, would somehow convert the suit into a suit being in rem. All these anomalies only highlight the impossibility of holding that an action instituted Under Section 31 of the Specific Relief Act, 1963 is an action in rem. [25]

The judgments of the District Court and the High Court in this case need no interference. This appeal, therefore, stands dismissed. [26]

Disposition: Appeal Dismissed

• • •

B. Santoshamma and Ors. vs. D. Sarala and Ors. (18.09.2020 – SC) : MANU/SC/0698/2020

Relative Section:

Code of Civil Procedure, 1908 (CPC) - Order II Rule 2, Code of Civil Procedure, 1908 (CPC) - Order II Rule 7, Code of Civil Procedure, 1908 (CPC) - Order VII Rule 11(d); Code of Civil Procedure, 1908 (CPC) - Section 21; Constitution of India - Article 136; Limitation Act, 1963 - Section 21, Limitation Act, 1963 - Section 21(1); Registration Act, 1908 - Section 17(1), Registration Act, 1908 - Section 18, Registration Act, 1908 - Section 50, Registration Act, 1908 - Section 50(1); Specific Relief Act 1963 - Section 10, Specific Relief Act 1963 - Section 11(2), Specific Relief Act 1963 - Section 12, Specific Relief Act 1963 - Section 14, Specific Relief Act 1963 - Section 16, Specific Relief Act 1963 - Section 34

Hon'ble Judges/Coram: U.U. Lalit and Indira Banerjee, JJ.

Equivalent Citation: 2020(6)BLJ247, 2020 (4) CCC 51 , 2021(2)CivilCC(S.C.), 2020(II)CLR(SC)754, 2021(3)ICC254, 2020/INSC/556, 2020(5)KLT645, 2021-1-LW435, (2021)1MLJ617, (2021)201PLR712, 2020(4)RCR(Civil)417, (2020)19SCC80, 2020 (7-8) SCJ 249, [2020]11SCR1

Number of Pages in the Original Judgment: 18

Case Reference:

Durga Prasad and Ors. v. Deep Chand and Ors. MANU/SC/0008/1953; Mahalaxmi Co-operative Housing Society Ltd. and Ors. v. Ashabhai Atmaram Patel (D) Th. L.Rs. and Ors. MANU/SC/0202/2013; Rikabdas A. Oswal v. Deepak Jewellers and Ors. MANU/SC/0993/1999; Dalip Singh v. Mehar Singh Rathee and Ors. MANU/SC/1337/2004 : (2004) 7 SCC 650

Case Note:

Civil - Suit for Specific Performance - Agreement to sell suit land between vendor and vendee -Challenge against Agreement alleged as time barred - Section 12 of the Specific Relief Act, 1963 - Section 21 of the Limitation Act, 1963 - Portion of suit land already sold prior to one 'P' by vendor - Vendor executed conveyance deed in favour of 'P' about portion of suit land after receiving full consideration from Vendee - Vendor later cited cancellation of agreement with Vendee on the ground of unwillingness to perform contract - By the time vendee decided to take action against 'P', proceedings also became time barred - Whether High Court erred in affirming the common judgment of the Trial Court whereby the Trial Court allowed the suit for specific performance in part, holding that the Vendee entitled to relief of specific performance in respect of 200 square yards of land covered by the Agreement?

Facts:

Vendor agreed to sell the entire suit land comprising 300 square yards to the Vendee for the consideration agreed. Vendee made part payment. Vendor although already had earlier sold 100 Sq. Yards out of said portion to 'P'. Vendor claimed to have informed Vendee about the transfer of land to 'P'. Vendee allegedly confirmed to manage 'P' for relinquishing said portion of suit land. However, later Vendor executed a registered deed of conveyance transferring portion of suit land in favour of 'P'. Vendee then was alleged of trying to interfere with 'P's possession of 100 sq. yards in the suit land. Trial Court allowed the suit in part holding that the Vendee, was not entitled to seek specific performance of the agreement in respect of 100 sq. yards but entitled to relief of specific performance in respect of the remaining area of the suit land. Vendors' defence that Vendee was unable and/or unwilling to perform her obligations under the agreement was rejected by the Trial Court and also the High Court. Appellant contended that the agreement between the Vendor and Vendee was liable to be cancelled as the Vendee had defaulted in making payment of the balance amount within the time stipulated in the said agreement. Hence, the present appeal

Held, while dismissing the Appeals:

The contention of the Vendor, that the agreement dated 21.3.1984 was subject to the condition that the Vendee would get the earlier agreement between the Vendor and 'P' not be accepted because this agreement does not incorporate any such condition. It was nowhere mentioned whether 'P' was ready to relinquish his rights under the said earlier agreement. 'P' denied knowledge of the agreement between the Vendor and the Vendee.Within a month and a few days from the date of execution of the agreement between the Vendor and the Vendee, after the Vendee tendered full consideration, the Vendor executed a registered deed of conveyance in favour of 'P' without any prior intimation to the Vendee, and without giving the Vendee any opportunity to persuade Pratap Reddy to abrogate his earlier agreement with the Vendor.[58]

It is well settled that the onus of proof lies on the party who makes an allegation. It was for the Vendor to establish that the agreement dated 21.3.1984 was subject to the condition as alleged by the Vendor, that the Vendee and/or her husband would negotiate with 'P to get his earlier agreement with the Vendor cancelled. The Vendor failed to discharge her onus of proving that there was such a condition in the agreement dated 21.3.1984. The Trial Court and the High Court rightly did not believe the Vendor.[59]

The relief of specific performance of an agreement, was at all material times, equitable, discretionary relief, governed by the provisions of the Specific Relief Act 1963. Even though the power of the Court to direct specific performance of an agreement may have been discretionary, such power could not be arbitrary. The discretion had necessarily to be exercised in accordance with sound and reasonable judicial principles.[67]

An agreement to sell immovable property, generally creates a right in personam in favour of the Vendee. The Vendee acquires a legitimate right to enforce specific performance of the agreement.[71]

It is well settled that the Court ordinarily enforces a contract in its entirety by passing a decree for its specific performance. However, Section 12 of the Specific Relief Act carves out exceptions, where the Court might direct specific performance of a contract in part. [72]

Where a party to the contract is unable to perform the whole of his part of the contract, the Court may, in the circumstances mentioned in Section 12 of the S.R.A., direct the specific performance of so much of the contract, as can be performed, particularly where the value of the part of the contract left unperformed would be small in proportion to the total value of the contract and admits of compensation.[73]

The Vendee claimed specific performance of the agreement dated 21.3.1984 in its entirety, and sought execution and registration of a deed of conveyance in respect of the entire suit land comprising 300 square yards, but without impleading 'P' to whom ownership of 100 square yards of land had been transferred by a registered deed of conveyance.[78]

A transferee to whom the subject matter of a sale agreement or part thereof is transferred, is a necessary party to a suit for specific performance. Unfortunately, the Vendee omitted to implead 'P'. By the time she filed an application to implead 'P', in 1989, the suit for specific performance of the agreement dated 21.3.1984 had become barred by limitation as against

'P'.[79]

Since title in respect of 100 square yards had passed to 'P' and the suit for specific performance was barred by limitation, the Trial Court was constrained to decree the suit for specific performance in part, and direct that a Deed of Conveyance be executed in respect of the balance 200 square yards of the suit land, under the ownership and control of the Vendor.[86]

Section 12 of the SRA is to be construed and interpreted in a purposive and meaningful manner to empower the Court to direct specific performance by the defaulting party, of so much of the contract, as can be performed, in a case like this. To hold otherwise would permit a party to a contract for sale of land, to deliberately frustrate the entire contract by transferring a part of the suit property and creating third party interests over the same.[87]

Appeals dismissed.[95]

• • •

CHAPTER XI

Jayakantham and Ors. vs. Abaykumar (21.02.2017 – SC) : MANU/SC/0193/2017

Relative Section:

Specific Relief Act 1963 - Section 20, Specific Relief Act 1963 - Section 20(1), Specific Relief Act 1963 - Section 20(2); Code of Civil Procedure, 1908 (CPC) - Section 100

Hon'ble Judges/Coram: Arun Mishra and Dr. D.Y. Chandrachud, JJ.

Equivalent Citation: 2017(172)AIC258, 2017 (121) ALR 895, 2017 2 AWC1729SC, 2017 (1) CCC 146 , 2017(1) CDR137(SC), 2017(2) CHN (SC) 12, 2017(2)CTC647, 2017(I)CLR(SC)682, 2017(I)ILR-CUT363, 2017/INSC/161, 2017(2)J.L.J.R.13, 2017-3-LW895, 2017(5)MhLj259, (2017)2MLJ460, 2017(3)MPLJ540, 2017(I)OLR818, 2017(2)PLJR191, (2017)187PLR830, 2017(2)RCR(Civil)104, 2017 135 RD727, 2017(3) SCALE61,(2017)5SCC178, 2017(2) SCJ449, [2017]2SCR355, (2017)4WBLR(SC)64, 2017 (1) WLN 175 (SC)

Number of Pages in the Original Judgment:7

Case Reference:

Parakunnan Veetill Joseph's Son Mathew v. Nedumbara Kuruvila's Son and Ors. MANU/SC/0173/1987 : AIR 1987 SC 2328; Sardar Singh v. Smt. Krishna Devi and Anr. MANU/SC/0102/1995 : (1994) 4 SCC 18; K. Narendra v. Riviera Apartments (P) Ltd. MANU/SC/0392/1999 : (1999) 5 SCC 77; Lourdu Mari David v. Louis Chinnaya Arogiaswamy; A.C. Arulappan v. Smt. Ahalya Naik MANU/SC/0438/2001 : (2001) 6 SCC 600; Nirmala Anand v. Advent Corporation (P) Ltd. and Ors. MANU/SC/0845/ 2002 : (2002) 8 SCC 146

Case Note:

Contract - Specific performance - Decreeing of suit - Trial Court decreed suit for specific performance instituted by Respondent against Appellants - Dismissing second appeal, Single Judge confirmed judgment of District Judge, by which appeal against judgment of Trial Court was dismissed - Hence, present appeal - Whether specific performance ought to have been decreed in present case

Facts:

The subject matter of the suit for specific performance was a property upon which a residential house was situated. An agreement to sell was entered into between the Appellants and the father of the Respondent. The consideration agreed upon was rupees one lakh sixty thousand of which an amount of rupees sixty thousand was received as advance. The balance was to be paid when the sale deed was executed. Time for completion of the sale transaction was reserved until 2 June 2002. A legal notice seeking performance of the agreement was issued on 7 May 2002. In response, the defence that was set up was inter alia that the agreement to sell was executed only as a security for a loan transaction. The Trial Court by a judgment and order decreed the suit for specific performance and directed the Appellants to execute a sale agreement in favour of the Respondent against receipt of the balance consideration of rupees one lakh. The Trial Court noted that the agreement to sell had been registered and rejected the defence that it was merely a document executed by way of security for a loan transaction. In the view of the Trial Court, there was nothing in the agreement to indicate that it was executed merely by way of a security. A finding of fact was arrived at to the effect that the Respondent was ready and willing to perform the agreement. The suit was decreed. The judgment of the Trial Court was confirmed in appeal by the District Judge. A second appeal was initially admitted on a substantial question of law but was eventually dismissed by the Single Judge of the High Court. Hence, the present appeal.

Held, while allowing the appeal:

(i) The court is not bound to grant the relief of specific performance merely because it is lawful to do so. Section 20(1) of the Specific Relief Act, 1963 indicates that the jurisdiction to decree specific performance is discretionary. Yet, the discretion of the court is not arbitrary but is "sound and reasonable", to be "guided by judicial principles". The exercise of discretion is capable of being corrected by a court of appeal in the hierarchy of appellate courts. Sub-section 2 of Section 20 contains a stipulation of those cases where the court may exercise its discretion not to grant specific performance. However, explanation 1 stipulates that the mere inadequacy of consideration, or the mere fact that the contract is onerous to the Defendant or improvident in its nature, will not constitute an unfair advantage within the meaning of Clause (a) or hardship within the meaning of Clause (b). Moreover, explanation 2 requires that the issue as to whether the performance of a contract involves hardship on the Defendant has to be determined with reference to the circumstances existing at the time of the contract, except where the hardship has been caused from an act of the Plaintiff subsequent to the contract. [8]

(ii) The terms of the contract, the conduct of parties at the time of entering into the agreement and circumstances under which the contract was entered into gave the Plaintiff an unfair advantage over the Defendants. These circumstances made it inequitable to enforce specific performance. A decree for the payment of compensation in lieu of specific performance would meet the ends of justice. The father of the Respondent paid an amount of rupees sixty thousand to the Appellants in June 1999 of the total agreed consideration of Rs. 1.60 lakhs. The Appellants voluntarily offered to pay an amount of rupees ten lakhs, as just compensation in lieu of specific performance. The ends of justice would be met by directing the Appellants to pay to the Respondent an amount of rupees fifteen lakhs in lieu of specific performance. The decree for specific performance shall accordingly stand set aside and shall stand substituted with a direction to the Appellants to pay a sum of rupees fifteen lakhs to the Respondent in lieu of specific performance. [11],[12] and[13]

Disposition: Appeal Allowed

• • •

Jaswinder Kaur (now deceased) through her L.Rs. and Ors. vs. Gurmeet Singh and Ors. (18.04.2017 – SC) : MANU/

Relative Section:

Urban Land Ceiling Act;Specific Relief Act 1963 - Section 12, Specific Relief Act 1963 - Section 12(1), Specific Relief Act 1963 - Section 12(2), Specific Relief Act 1963 - Section 12(3), Specific Relief Act 1963 - Section 12(4), Specific Relief Act 1963 - Section 13, Specific Relief Act 1963 - Section 14, Specific Relief Act 1963 - Section 16, Specific Relief Act 1963 - Section 17, Specific Relief Act 1963 - Section 20; Code of Civil Procedure, 1908 (CPC)

Hon'ble Judges/Coram: Arun Mishra and Amitava Roy, JJ.

Equivalent Citation:2017(176)AIC129,2017(123)ALR808,2017(6)CTC614,2017(II)CLR(SC) 279, 2017-4-LW258, 2017(2)RCR(Civil)891, 2017 137 RD269, 2017(6)SCALE86, (2017)12SCC810, [2017] 5SCR430

Number of Pages in the Original Judgment: 11

Case Reference:

William Graham v. Krishna Chandra Dey MANU/PR/0011/1924 : AIR 1925 PC 45; Abdul Haq v. Mohammad Yehia Khan and Ors. MANU/BH/0317/1923 : AIR 1924 Pat. 81; Abdul Rahim and Ors. v. Tufan Gazi and Ors. MANU/WB/0083/1928 : AIR 1928 Cal. 584; Surjit Kaur v. Naurata Singh and Anr. MANU/SC/0570/2000 : 2000 (7) SCC 379

Case Note:

Contract - Specific performance - Readiness and willingness - Respondents/Plaintiffs filed suit for specific performance of agreement to sale - Or in alternative, refund of earnest money with interest and damages - Trial Court held that Plaintiffs were not ready and willing to perform their part of agreements - Appellants/Defendants cancelled agreement and forfeited earnest money - Thus, Plaintiffs could not be said to be entitled to specific performance of agreement - Plaintiffs preferred First Appeal - First Appellate Court concluded that Plaintiffs were not ready and willing to perform their part of agreement - Neither they had required balance amount for purchase of property in question as per agreements - High Court decreed suit partly - It observed at one go that readiness and willingness had to be seen from conduct of parties - Suit of Plaintiffs was partly decreed by granting specific performance of agreement to sell - Hence, present appeal - Whether impugned judgment and decree passed by High Court was sustainable

Facts:

An agreement was entered into, in which it was agreed that for the sum of Rs. 55,00,000/-, Appellants/Defendants would sell the property. A sum of Rs. 50,000/- was paid as earnest money. Later on, at the time of payment of Rs. 14,50,000/- further agreement was entered into which was also reduced in writing in which it was stipulated that sale deed would be executed by 30.10.1990. It would be open to the Respondents/Plaintiffs to construct boundary wall between 24.4.1990 to 15.5.1990 at their own cost and the possession of the land would be delivered at the time of registration of the sale deed. This agreement referred the prior agreement on which date a sum of Rs. 50,000/- had been paid as earnest money. The land had been mortgaged with the Bank. It would be necessary for the Defendants to clear the amount and to obtain No objection Certificate from the Bank and only thereafter sale deed to be executed.

The Plaintiffs filed suit for specific performance of the agreement to sale or in alternative, refund of earnest money with interest and damages were claimed. The Trial Court held that the Plaintiffs were not ready and willing to perform their part of the agreements. Defendants cancelled the agreement and forfeited the earnest money. Thus, the Plaintiffs could not be said to be entitled to specific performance of the agreement. It was also found that the Plaintiffs were not having the required money in order to purchase the property. The Plaintiffs preferred First Appeal. The First Appellate Court (FAC) also examined the evidence of the Plaintiffs in extenso and the legality of the findings recorded by the Trial Court and came to the conclusion that Plaintiffs were not ready and willing to perform their part of the agreement neither they were having the required balance amount for the purchase of the property in question as per the agreements.

The High Court without discussing evidence and the correctness of the findings as recorded by the Trial court and affirmed by the FAC had referred to Section 12 of the Specific Relief Act, 1963 (the Act) and on the ground that a sum of Rs. 15, 00,000/- had been accepted by the Defendants decreed the suit partly. It observed at one go that the readiness and willingness had to be seen from the conduct of the parties. The High Court partly modified the judgments and decrees of both the Courts below. The suit of the Plaintiffs was partly decreed by granting specific performance of the agreement to sell viz-à-viz the area for which sale consideration of Rs. 14,50,000/- had been paid and relief of specific performance qua other area was declined, much less findings of the Courts below are affirmed. Hence, the present appeal.

Held, while partly allowing the appeal:

(i) The High court could not have decreed the suit without reversing the finding recorded by the Trial Court and affirmed by the First Appellate Court on elaborate discussion of the evidence and the deposition of the Plaintiffs himself to the effect that Plaintiffs were not ready and willing to purchase the property as projected from their conduct. The Defendants had got the property redeemed from the Bank and the factum of redemption had been intimated to the Plaintiffs by serving notices.No positive finding had been recorded by the High Court with respect to readiness and willingness of the Plaintiffs merely by making payment of part consideration it could not have inferred. It was not within the jurisdiction of the High Court to decree the suit for specific performance on the basis of the elementary principles relating to specific performance as envisaged under the Act. [13] and[14]

(ii) When they had entered into an agreement, the Defendants had clearly disclosed to the Plaintiffs that as a matter of fact the property had been mortgaged with the Bank. It was for the Plaintiffs to ascertain whether the Defendants were owner or not before entering into agreement. The stand of the Plaintiff was unsound and unworthy of credence and they had tried to take guise of defects of the title of the property in untenable manner. The Trial Court as well as the FAC had also found that in spite of the notice given by the Defendants to the Plaintiffs to be present for the execution of the sale deed in office of Sub-Registrar none of the Plaintiffs was present in the office of the Sub Registrar on the date on which the sale deed had to be executed. It showed that they were not ready and willing to purchase the property in spite of the notice having been given by the Defendants to them to keep them present for the execution of the sale deed on the stipulated date of the agreement failing which the earnest money had to be forfeited. [16] and[17]

(iii) Section 12 of the Act makes it clear that it is not open to the High Court to direct specific performance of a part of contract except otherwise provided in the Section in absence any of the exigencies available under the provisions of Sub-Sections 2, 3, and 4 of Section 12 so as to decree the suit. The High Court could not have decreed the suit with an purview of Section 12. If a party is not ready and willing to perform whole of the contract, specific performance with respect to the part of the contract could not have been ordered in view of the aforesaid decision and Section 16 (c) of the Act. In the instant case, the High Court ignored basic principles that the party cannot claim specific performance. [19] and[24]

(iv) As earnest money had been paid i.e. initially Rs. 50,000/- and subsequently advance of Rs. 14,50,000/-. The forfeiture of the amount paid as earnest money of Rs. 50,000/- had rightly been made as Plaintiffs were delaying to perform their essential part of contract which was enjoined upon them. Remaining money paid in advance was ordered to be refunded with simple interest to the Plaintiffs. However, the Plaintiffs shall bear the cost of the Appellants of courts below and the cost of the appeal. The impugned judgment and the decree passed by the High Court was set aside. [25] and[26]

Prior History / High Court Status: From the Order dated 17.02.2016 of the High Court of Punjab & Haryana at Chandigarh in RSA No. 3038 of 2010 (MANU/PH/0224/2016)

Disposition: Appeal Partly Allowed

• • •

Hemanta Mondal and Ors. vs. Ganesh Chandra Naskar (23.09.2015 – SC) : MANU/SC/1070/2015

Relative Section: Specific Relief Act 1963 - Section 20,Section 20(2), Section 20(3)

Hon'ble Judges/Coram: Dipak Misra and Prafulla C. Pant, JJ.

Equivalent Citation: 2015(155)AIC10, AIR2015SC3757, 2016(1)AJR531, 2015(6)ALD133(SC), 2015 (113) ALR 716, 2015(II)CLR(SC)888, 2016-3-LW210, 2016(6)MhLj30, 2016(4)MPLJ254,2015(4)RCR (Civil) 599,2016130RD443,2015(10)SCALE1,(2016)1SCC567,2016(6)SCJ515, [2015]9SCR300,(2016) 1WBLR(SC)1

Number of Pages in the Original Judgment: 6

Case Reference: nil

Case Note:

Contract - Specific performance of contract - Agreement to sell land - Favour of Plaintiff - Earnest money paid - Rest to be paid - Execution of sale deed - Measurements made - Amount of consideration found - Plaintiff willing to pay balance amount - Defendant declined execution - Offered to pay back earnest money - Suit for specific performance -Disposed of by Trial Court - Defendant directed - Refund earnest money - Plaintiff challenged said judgment - First Appellate Court - Directed execution - Second appeal by Defendants - High Court - Modified decree of first Appellate Court - Decree of specific performance affirmed in respect of agreement - Not on basis of measurement - Matter remanded - Defendants filed appeal - Whether in the facts and circumstances of the case, a decree of specific performance of agreement of sale should have been passed - Whether decree of refund of part consideration received by the Defendant, with interest, would have served the ends of justice

Facts:

As per the agreement dated 04.02.1992, Defendant (Mishrilal Mondal) agreed to sell the land in favour of Plaintiff (Ganesh Chandra Naskar), and received some amount as earnest money, and rest of the consideration was to be paid at the time of the execution of sale deed. As per plaintiff, the measurements were made by surveyors in the presence of parties, and amount of consideration for entire area of land was also found. It is pleaded that Plaintiff was/is always ready and willing to pay balance amount to get the sale deed executed, but the Defendant declined to execute the same. On this, the Plaintiff gave notice to the Defendant to execute the sale deed but he questioned the correctness of the measurements, and offered to pay back the earnest money. Consequently, the suit for specific performance, possession and injunction was filed by the Plaintiff.

During the pendency of suit due to the death of the original Defendant his heirs were substituted. The Trial Court disposed of the suit directing the Defendant to refund the earnest money to the Plaintiff. Said judgment and decree was challenged by the plaintiff in Title appeal which was allowed and the first Appellate Court directed the Defendant to execute sale deed after accepting balance amount.

Defendants challenged the said judgment and decree in Second Appeal. The High Court, while modifying the decree passed by first Appellate Court, directed that the decree of specific performance shall stand affirmed in respect of agreement but not on basis of measurement. The High Court remanded the matter to first appellate court, with further direction that the Defendant shall be allowed to apply for appointment of a Commissioner for doing the survey of the land to be transferred. It is also clarified by the High Court that if no such application is moved the suit shall stand decreed, as per the measurements made by surveyors. Unsatisfied with the modified decree, passed by High Court, the Defendants are before us, in this appeal, through special leave.

Held, while disposing of the appeal

(I) Having heard learned Counsel for the parties, we are not inclined to interfere with the findings affirmed by the High Court. On consideration of submissions of rival parties in the present appeal the only point before us is whether in the facts and circumstances of the case, a decree of specific performance of agreement of sale should have been passed, or the decree of refund of part consideration received by the Defendant, with interest, would have served the ends of justice.[14]

(II) Section 20 of Specific Relief Act, 1963 gives discretion to the court, and provides that the court is not bound to grant relief of specific performance merely because it is lawful to do so. It further provides that the discretion is not to be exercised arbitrarily but guided by judicial principles. Sub-section (3) provides that court may properly exercise discretion to decree specific performance in any case where Plaintiff has done substantial acts or suffered losses in consequence of a contract capable of specific performance.[15]

(III) In the present case, it appears that possession was not given to the Plaintiff at the time of execution of the agreement, nor the area of land agreed to be sold was clear, as such, it cannot be said that the Plaintiff has done substantial acts or suffered losses due to expenditure in constructions etc., in consequence of a contract capable of specific performance. The direction given by High Court in the impugned order shows that the measurements of land actually agreed to be sold, are not final. In the above facts and circumstances of the case, we are of the view that instead of affirming the decree of specific performance as modified by High Court, it will be equitable, just and proper to direct the Appellants to pay back the earnest money accepted by the original Defendant with interest @ 18% per annum to the Plaintiff/Respondent from 04.02.1992 till date, within a period of three months from today, failing which this appeal shall stand dismissed.[16] and[17]

• • •

CHAPTER XIV

Bharat Aluminium Company and Ors. vs. Kaiser Aluminium Technical Service, Inc. and Ors. (06.09.2012 – SC) : MANU/SC/0722/2012

Relative Section:

Arbitration Act, 1940 [repealed] - Section 15, Arbitration Act, 1940 [repealed] - Section 16, Arbitration Act, 1940 [repealed] - Section 30, Arbitration Act, 1940 [repealed] - Section 34; Arbitration And Conciliation Act, 1996 - Section 1, Arbitration And Conciliation Act, 1996 - Section 1(2),Section 10 to Section 26,Arbitration And Conciliation Act, 1996 - Section 11(12), Section 11(9), Section 2(1),Section 2(1) (e), Section 2(1)(e), Section 2(1)(f), Section 2(2), Section 2(3), Section 2(4), Section 2(5),Section 2(7),Section 2(i)(a), Section 20(1), Section 20(2), Section 20(3), Section 27, Section 28 to Section 33, Section 28(1),Section 28(1) (b),Section 28(1)(a), Section 34, Section 34(2)(iv), Section 35 to Section 49, Arbitration And Conciliation Act, 1996 - Section 48(1), Arbitration And Conciliation Act, 1996 - Section 48(1)(e), Arbitration And Conciliation Act, 1996 - Section 48(3), Arbitration And Conciliation Act, 1996 - Section 5, Arbitration And Conciliation Act, 1996 - Section 50, to Section 54, Arbitration And Conciliation Act, 1996 - Section 6, Arbitration And Conciliation Act, 1996 - Section 67, Arbitration And Conciliation Act, 1996 - Section 68, Arbitration And Conciliation Act, 1996 - Section 69, Arbitration And Conciliation Act, 1996 - Section 69 (1), Arbitration And Conciliation Act, 1996 - Section 7 to Section 9, Arbitration And Conciliation Act, 1996 - Section 82(1)

Code of Civil Procedure, 1908 (CPC) - Order II Rule 1; Order VII Rule 1; Order VII Rule 1(e); Order VII Rule 11; Order VII Rule 11(a); Order VII Rule 11a; Order XI Rule 1(1); Order XI Rule 1(1)(i); Order XI Rule 1(i);

Code of Civil Procedure, 1908 (CPC) - Section 151,Section 9; Section 94;

Constitution Of India - Article 243, Constitution Of India - Article 245;

Indian Contract Act, 1872 - Section 23, Indian Contract Act, 1872 - Section 28;

Specific Relief Act 1963 - Section 14(2), Specific Relief Act 1963 - Section 37, Section 38

Hon'ble Judges/Coram:

S.H. Kapadia, C.J.I., Devinder Kumar Jain, S.S. Nijjar, Ranjana Prakash Desai and J.S. Khehar, JJ.

Equivalent Citation:

2012(3)ARBLR515(SC), 2013 1 AWC463SC, [2012]110CLA293(SC), [2013]180CompCas311(SC), (2012) 4 CompLJ345(SC), (2012)4CompLJ345(SC), 2012(5)CTC615, JT2012(9)SC105, JT2012(9)SC27, 2013(1) RCR (Civil)1, 2012(8)SCALE333, (2012)9SCC552, [2012]12SCR327

Number of Pages in the Original Judgment: 70

Case Reference:

Bhatia International v. Bulk Trading S.A. and Anr. MANU/SC/0185/ 2002 : (2002) 4 SCC 105 : (2004) 2 SCC 105; Venture Global Engineering v. Satyam Computer Services Ltd. and Anr. MANU/SC/0333/2008 : 2008 (1) Scale 214 : 2008 (4) SCC 190; Konkan Railway Corporation Ltd. and Anr. v. Rani Construction Pvt. Ltd. MANU/SC/0053/2002 : (2002) 2 SCC 388; SBP and Co. v. Patel Engineering Ltd. and Anr. MANU/SC/1787/ 2005 : (2005) 8 SCC 618; Nalinakhya Bysack v. Shyam Sunder Haldar and Ors. MANU/SC/0076/1953 : 1953 SCR 533; Magor and St. Mellons RDC v. Newport Corporation 1951 (2) All ER 839; Duport Steels Ltd. v. Sirs (1980) 1 All ER 529; National Thermal Power Corporation v. Singer Co. and Ors. MANU/SC/0146/1993 : (1992) 3 SCC 551; Reliance Industries Ltd. v. Enron Oil and Gas India Ltd. 2002 (1) Lloyd Law Reports 645; Braes of Doune Wind Farm (Scotland) Limited v. Alfred McAlpine Business Services Limited (2008) EWHC 426 (TCC); Shashoua and Ors. v. Sharma (2009) EWHC 957 (Comm.); Siskina (Cargo Owners) v. Distos Compania Navieria SA 1979 AC 210; Fourie v. Le Roux 2007 (1) WLR 320 : 2007 (1) All ER 1087; Adhunik Steels Ltd. v. Orissa Manganese and Minerals Pvt. Ltd. MANU/SC/2936/2007 : 2007 (7) SCC 125, 136; State of Orissa v. Madan Gopal Rungta MANU/SC/0012/1951 : 1952(1) SCR 28 : AIR 1952 SC 12; U.P. Junior Doctors' Action Committee v. Dr. B. Sheetal Nandwani 1997 Suppl (1) SCC 680; State of Uttar Pradesh v. Ram Sukhi Devi MANU/SC/ 0980/2004 : (2005) (9) SCC 733; Deoraj v. State of Maharashtra and Ors. MANU/SC/0314/2004 : (2004) 4 SCC 697; Raja Khan v. Uttar Pradesh Sunni Central Wakf Board and Ors. (2011) 2 SCC 741; ONGC v. Western Co. of North America MANU/SC/0014/1987 : 1987 (1) SCC 496; ABC Laminart Pvt. Ltd. v. A.P. Agencies, Salem MANU/SC/0001/1989 : 1989 (2) SCC 163; Interglobe Aviation Ltd. v. N. Satchidanand MANU/SC/0799/

2011 : 2011 (7) SCC 463; TDM Infrastructure Pvt. Ltd. v. U.E. Development India Pvt. Ltd. MANU/SC/2263/2008 : 2008 (14) SCC 271; Guru Nanak Foundation v. Rattan Singh and Sons. MANU/SC/0001/1981 : 1981 (4) SCC 634; Commissioner for Special Purpose of Income Tax v. Premsel LR (1891) AC 531, 549; Crawford v. Spooner 6 Moo PC 1 : 4 MIA 179; Hansraj Gupta v. Official Liquidator of Dehra Dun-Mussoorie Electric Tramway Co., Ltd. MANU/PR/0062/1932 : (1933) LR 60 IA 13 : AIR (1933) PC 63; Naviera Amazonica Peruana S.A. v. Compania Internacionale De Seguros Del Peru 1988 (1) Lloyd's Law Reports 116; Union of India v. McDonnell Douglas Corporation 1993 (3) Lloyd's Law Reports 48; Umed v. Raj Singh MANU/SC/0278/1974 : 1975 (1) SCC 76, 103; Hill v. William Hill (Park Lane) Ltd. 1949 AC 530, 546; Bergesen v. Joseph Muller Corporation 710 F.2d 928; James Miller and Partners v. Whitworth Street Estates (Manchester) Ltd. (1970) 1 Lloyd's Rep. 269 : (1970) A.C. 583; C v. D (2007) EWCA Civ 1282 (CA); Sulamerica CIA Nacional de Seguros SA v. Enesa Engenharia SA - Enesa 2012 WL 14764; Black Clawsen International Limited v. Papierirke Waldhof-Aschaffenburg AG (1981) 2 LLR 446, 453; Chanel Tunnel Group Limited v. Balfour Beatty Construction Limited (1993) 1 LLR 291 : (1993) AC 334; A v. B (2007) 1 Lloyds Report 237; R.S. Raghnath v. State of Karnataka and Anr. MANU/SC/0012/1992 : (1992) 1 SCC 335; Karaha Bodas Co. LLC v. Perusahaan Pertambangan Minyak Dan Gas Bumi Negara 335 F.3d 357; Karaha Bodas Co. LLC (Cayman Islands) v. Perusahaan Pertambangan Minyak Dan Gas Bumi Negara - Pertamina (Indonesia) Yearbook Comm. Arb'n Vol. XXVIII) 2003) 752; International Electric Corporation v. Bridas Sociedad Anonima Petroleva, Industrial Y Commercial 745 F Supp 172, 178 (SDNY 1990); International Standard Electric Corporation (US) v. Bridas Sociedad Anonima Petrolera (Argentina) (1992) VII Ybk Comm Arb 639; Investors Compensation Scheme Ltd. v. West Bromwich Building Society (1998) WLR 1896 913; Bank of Credit and Commerce International SA v. Ali and Ors. (2001) 2 WLR 735 749; Seaford Court Estates Ld. v. Asher; Punjab Land Development and Reclamation Corporation Ltd., Chandigarh v. Presiding Officer, Labour Court, Chandigarh and Ors. MANU/SC/0479/1990 : (1990) 3 SCC 682; Corocraft Ltd. v. Pan American Airways All ER 1071 D WLR 732; State of Haryana v. Sampuran Singh AIR 1957; Gwalior Rayon Silk Mfg. (Wvg.) Co. Ltd. v. Custodian of Vested Forests MANU/SC/0308/ 1990 : AIR 1990 SC 1747, 1752; Cotton Corporation Limited v. United Industrial Bank MANU/SC/0375/1983 : (1983) 4 SCC 625; Ashok Kumar

Lingala v. State of Karnataka MANU/SC/1260/2011 : (2012) 1 SCC 321; Bharati Shipyard Ltd. Vs. Ferrostaal AG & Anr., SLP (C) No. 27824 of 2011

Case Note:

(1) Arbitration and Conciliation Act, 1996 - Parts I and II and Section 2(2)--Applicability of Act--Section 2(2) makes declaration that Part I of Act--To apply to all arbitrations taking place within India--Hence, Part I would have to application to International Commercial Arbitration held outside India--Accordingly, in foreign seated international commercial arbitration--No application for interim relief would be maintainable under Section 9 or any other provision--Similarly, no suit for interim injunction simplicitor--Would be maintainable in India--On basis of international commercial arbitration with seat outside India--However, law declared herein to apply prospectively to all arbitration agreements executed hereafter.

The Arbitration and Conciliation Act, 1996 has accepted the territoriality principle which has been adopted in the U.N.C.I.T.R.A.L. Model Law. Section 2(2) makes a declaration that Part I of the Arbitration Act, 1996 shall apply to all arbitrations which take place within India. Accordingly, Part I of the Arbitration Act, 1996 would have no application to International Commercial Arbitration held outside India. Therefore, such awards would only be subject to the jurisdiction of the Indian courts when the same are sought to be enforced in India in accordance with the provisions contained in Part II of the Arbitration Act, 1996. Accordingly, the provisions contained in Arbitration Act, 1996 make it crystal clear that there can be no overlapping or intermingling of the provisions contained in Part I with the provisions contained in Part II of the Arbitration Act, 1996.

The provision contained in Section 2(2) of the Arbitration Act, 1996 is not in conflict with any of the provisions either in Part I or in Part II of the Arbitration Act, 1996. In a foreign seated international commercial arbitration, no application for interim relief would be maintainable under Section 9 or any other provision, as applicability of Part I of the Arbitration Act, 1996 is limited to all arbitrations which take place in India, Similarly, no suit for interim injunction simplicitor would be maintainable in India, on the basis of an international commercial arbitration with a seat outside India.

(2) Arbitration and Conciliation Act, 1996--Section 9--Interim measures under Section 9--Not to be granted in arbitrations taking place outside India.

There is no existing provision under the C.P.C. or under the Arbitration Act, 1996 for a Court to grant interim measures in terms of Section 9, in arbitrations which take place outside India, even though the parties by agreement may have made the Arbitration Act, 1996 as the governing law of arbitration.

The provision contained in Section 9 is limited in its application to arbitrations which take place in India. Extending the applicability of Section 9 to arbitrations which take place outside India would be to do violence to the policy of the territoriality declared in Section 2(2) of the Arbitration Act, 1996.

(3) Specific Relief Act, 1963--Section 14(2)--Arbitration--Suit barred under Section 14(2) in arbitration matters.

In matters pertaining to arbitration, the suit would also be barred under Section 14(2) of the Specific Relief Act, 1963. Although the provision exists in Section 37 of the Specific Relief Act, 1963, for grant of temporary/ perpetual injunction, but the existence of cause of action would be essential under this provision also. Similar would be the position under Section 38 of the Specific Relief Act.

(4) Code of Civil Procedure, 1908--Section 9 and Order VII, Rule 11(a)-- Arbitration and Conciliation Act, 1996--Sections 8 and 45--Suit--Pendency of arbitration proceedings outside India--Would not provide cause of action for suit--Where main prayer is injunction.

endency of the arbitration proceedings outside India would not provide a cause of action for a suit where the main prayer is for injunction. Mr. Sundaram has rightly pointed out that the entire suit would be based on the pendency of arbitration proceedings in a foreign country. Therefore, it would not be open to a party to file a suit touching on the merits of the arbitration. If such a suit was to be filed, it would in all probabilities he stayed in view of Sections 8 and 45 of the Arbitration Act, 1996. It must also be noticed that such a suit, if at all, can only be framed as a suit to "inter alia restrain the defendant from parting with property." Now, if the right to such property could possibly arise, only if the future arbitration award could possibly be in favour of the plaintiff, no suit for a declaration could obviously be filed, based purely only on such a contingency. All that could then be filed would, therefore, be a bare suit for injunction restraining the other party from parting with property. The interlocutory relief would also be identical. Therefore, such a suit would not be maintainable, because an interlocutory injunction can only be granted during the pendency of a civil suit claiming a relief which is likely to result in a final decision upon the subject in dispute. The suit would be maintainable only on the existence of a cause of action, which would entitle the plaintiff for the substantive relief claimed in the suit. The interim injunction itself must be a part of the substantive relief to which the plaintiff's cause of action entitled him. But, most of the aforesaid ingredients are missing in a suit claiming injunction restraining a party from dealing with the assets during the pendency of arbitration proceedings outside India. Since the dispute is to be decided by the Arbitrator, no substantive relief concerning the merits, of the arbitration could be claimed in the suit. The only relief that could be asked for would be to safeguard the property which the plaintiff may or may not be entitled to proceed against. In fact the plaintiffs only claim would depend on the outcome of the arbitration proceeding in a foreign country over which the courts in India would have no jurisdiction. The cause of action would clearly be contingent/speculative. There would be no existing cause of action. The plaint itself would be liable to be rejected under Order VII, Rule 11(a). In any event, no interim relief could be granted unless it is in aid of and ancillary to the main relief that may be available to a party on final determination of rights in a suit.

(5) Arbitration and Conciliation Act, 1996--Section 48(1)(e)--Foreign award falling under Part II of Act--Indian Courts cannot annul international commercial award made outside India.

The intention of the Legislature is clear that the Court may refuse to enforce the foreign award on satisfactory proof of any of the grounds mentioned in Section 48(1), by the party resisting the enforcement of the award. The provision sets out the defences open to the party to resist enforcement of a foreign award. The words "suspended or set aside", in Clause (e) of Section 48(1) cannot be interpreted to mean that, by necessary implication, the foreign award sought to be enforced in India can also be challenged on merits in Indian Courts. The provision merely recognizes that courts of the two nations which are competent to annul or suspend an award. It does not ipso facto confer jurisdiction on such Courts for annulment of an award made outside the country. Such jurisdiction has to be specifically provided, in the relevant national legislation of the country in which the Court concerned is located. So far as India is concerned, the Arbitration Act, 1996 does not confer any such jurisdiction on the Indian Courts to annul an international commercial award made outside India. Such provision exists in Section 34, which is placed in Part I. Therefore, the applicability of that provision is limited to the awards made in India. If the arguments of the counsel for the appellants are accepted, it would entail incorporating the provision contained in Section 34 of the Arbitration Act, 1996, which is placed in Part I of the Arbitration Act, 1996 into Part II of the said Act. This is not permissible as the intention of the Parliament was clearly to confine the powers of the Indian Courts to set aside an award relating to international commercial arbitrations, which take place in India.

(6) Arbitration and Conciliation Act, 1996--Section 45--Non-obstante clause in Section 45--Does not indicate that provisions of Part I of Act-- Would also be applicable to arbitrations taking place outside India.

(7) Arbitration and Conciliation Act, 1996--Part I and Part II--Having accepted principle of territoriality--Evident that intention of Parliament-- Was to segregate Part I and Part II--Any provisions contained in Part I-- Cannot be made applicable to foreign awards--It cannot be contended that provisions contained in Part II--Are supplementary to provision contained in Part I--Parliament clearly segregated two parts.

(8) Arbitration and Conciliation Act, 1996--Section 28--Section 28 merely shows that Legislature segregated domestic and international arbitration.

Section 28 of Arbitration and Conciliation Act, 1996, merely shows that the Legislature has segregated the domestic and international arbitration. Therefore, to suit India, conflict of law rules have been suitably modified, where the arbitration is in India. This will not apply where the seat is outside India. In that event, the conflict of laws rules of the country in which the arbitration takes place would have to be applied. Therefore, the emphasis placed on the expression "where the place of arbitration is situated in India", by the senior counsel for the appellants, is not indicative of the fact that the intention of Parliament was to give an extra-territorial operation to Part I of the Arbitration Act 1996.

(9) Arbitration and Conciliation Act, 1996--Sections 2(2), 20 and Part I--Scope of Section 20--Section has to be read in context of Section 2(2)-- Placing threshold limitation of applicability of Part I--Where place of arbitration is in India--Hence, Section 20 would also not support submissions of extra-territoriality of Part I.

(10) Arbitration and Conciliation Act, 1996--Section 2(1)(e) and 20-- Expression "court"--Meaning and extent--Provision contained in Section 2(1)(e) being purely jurisdictional in nature--Can have no relevance to question--Whether Part I of Act applies to arbitrations taking place outside

India.

The term "subject-matter of the arbitration" cannot be confused with 'subject-matter of the suit" as used in Section 2(1)(e) of Arbitration and Conciliation Act, 1996. The term "subject-matter" in Section 2(1)(e) is confined to Part I. It has a reference and connection with the process of dispute resolution. Its purpose is to identify the courts having supervisory control over the arbitration proceedings. Hence, it refers to a court which would essentially be a court of the seat of the arbitration process. Therefore, the provision in Section 2(1)(e) has to be construed keeping in view the provisions in Section 20 which give recognition to party autonomy. Accepting the narrow construction as projected by the counsel for the appellants would, in fact, render Section 20 nugatory. Therefore, the Legislature has intentionally given jurisdiction to two courts, i.e., the court which would have jurisdiction where the cause of action is located and the courts where the arbitration takes place. This was necessary as on many occasions the agreement may provide for a seat of arbitration at a place which would be neutral to both the parties. Therefore, the courts where the arbitration takes place would be required to exercise supervisory control over the arbitral process. For example, if the arbitration is held in Delhi, where neither of the parties are from Delhi, (Delhi having been chosen as a neutral place as between a party from Mumbai and the other from Kolkata) and the Tribunal sitting in Delhi passes an interim order under Section 17 of the Arbitration Act, 1996, the appeal against such an interim order under Section 37 must. He to the Courts of Delhi being the Courts having supervisory jurisdiction over the arbitration proceedings and the Tribunal. This would be irrespective of the fact that the obligations to be performed under the contract were to be performed either at Mumbai or at Kolkata, and only arbitration is to take place in Delhi. In such circumstances, both the Courts would have jurisdiction, i.e., the Court within whose jurisdiction the subject-matter of the suit is situated and the courts within the jurisdiction of which the dispute resolution, i.e., arbitration is located.

The definition of Section 2(1)(e) includes "subject-matter of the arbitration" to give jurisdiction to the courts where the arbitration takes place, which otherwise would not exist. On the other hand, Section 47 which is in Part II of the Arbitration Act 1996 dealing with enforcement of certain foreign awards has defined the term "court" as a court having jurisdiction over the subject-matter of the award. This has a clear reference to a court within whose jurisdiction the asset/person is located, against which/whom the enforcement of the international arbitral award is sought. The provisions contained in Section 2(1)(e) being purely jurisdictional in nature can have no relevance to the question whether Part I applies to arbitrations which take place outside India.

(11) Arbitration and Conciliation Act, 1996--Section 2(7)--Section 2(7) does not in any manner relax territorial principle--Adopted by Act.

Section 2(7) of Arbitration and Conciliation Act, 1996, defining domestic award does not, in any manner, relax the territorial principle adopted by Arbitration Act, 1996. It certainly does not introduce the concept of a delocalized arbitration into the Arbitration Act. 1996. It must be remembered that Part I of the Arbitration Act, 1996 applies not only to purely domestic arbitrations, i.e., where none of the parties are in any way "foreign" but also to "international commercial arbitrations" covered within Section 2(1)(f) held in India. The term "domestic award" can be used in two senses: one to distinguish it from "international award", and the other to distinguish it from a "foreign award". It must also be remembered that "foreign award" may well be a domestic award in the country in which it is rendered. As the whole of the Arbitration Act, 1996 is designed to give different treatments to the awards made in India and those made outside India, the distinction is necessarily to be made between the terms "domestic awards" and "foreign awards". The Scheme of the Arbitration Act, 1996 provides that Part I shall apply to both "international arbitrations" which take place in India as well as "domestic arbitrations" which would normally take place in India. This is clear from a number of provisions contained in the Arbitration Act. 1996 viz. the Preamble of the said Act; proviso and the Explanation to Section 1(2); Sections 2(1)(f); 11(9), 11(12); 28(1)(a) and 28(1)(b). All the aforesaid provisions, which incorporate the term "international", deal with pre-award situation. The term "international award" does not occur in Part I at all. Therefore, it would appear that the term "domestic award" means an award made in India whether in a purely domestic context, i.e., domestically rendered award in a domestic arbitration or in the international context, i.e., domestically rendered award in an international arbitration, Both the types of awards are liable to be challenged under Section 34 and are enforceable under Section 36 of the Arbitration Act, 1996. Therefore, it seems clear that the object of Section 2(7) is to distinguish the domestic award covered under Part I of the Arbitration Act, 1996 from the "foreign award" covered under Part II of the aforesaid Act; and not to distinguish the "domestic award" from an "international award" rendered in India. In other words, the provision highlights, if any thing, a clear distinction between Part I and Part II as being applicable in completely different fields and with no overlapping provisions.

(12) Arbitration and Conciliation Act, 1996--Sections 2(2), 2(4) and 2(5)--Section 2(2) would not be applicable to arbitrations held outside India--No conflict at all between Section 2(2) on one hand--And Sections 2(4) and 2(5) on other hand.

There is no conflict at all between Section 2(2) on the one hand and Sections 2(4) and 2(5) on the other hand.

The provisions of Section 2(4) and Section 2(5) would not be applicable to arbitrations which are covered by Part II of the Arbitration Act, 1996, i.e., the arbitrations which take place outside India. Therefore, there is no inconsistency between Sections 2(2), 2(4) and 2(5).

Bhatia International, (2002) 4 SCC 105, not approved.

(13) Arbitration and Conciliation Act, 1996--Section 2(2) and Part I--Omission of word "only" in Section 2(2)--Does not detract from territorial scope of its application--As embodied in Article 1(2) of Model Law.

Omission of the word "only" in Section 2(2) of, the Arbitration Act 1996 does not detract from the territorial scope of its application as embodied in Article 1(2) of the Model Law. The article merely states that the Arbitration Law as enacted in a given state shall apply if the arbitration is in the territory of that State. The absence of the word "only" which is found in Article 1(2) of the Model Law, from Section 2(2) of the Arbitration Act, 1996 does not change the content/import of Section 2(2) as limiting the application of Part I of the Arbitration Act, 1996 to arbitrations where the place/seat is in India.

Bhatia International (supra) and Venture Global Engineering (supra) holding that Part I of Arbitration Act, 1996 would also apply to arbitrations not taking place in India, not approved.

Ratio Decidendi:

"Courts shall not interfere with any established interpretation of statute unless there is certain error apparent in implementation of such interpretation."

Facts:

1.Since the issue raised in the reference is pristinely legal, it is not necessary to make any detailed reference to the facts of the appeal. We may, however, notice the very essential facts leading to the filing of the appeal. An agreement dated 22nd April, 1993 was executed between the

Appellant and the Respondent, under which the Respondent was to supply and install a computer based system for Shelter Modernization at Balco's Korba Shelter. The agreement contained an arbitration clause for resolution of disputes arising out of the contract. The arbitration clause contained in Articles 17 and 22 was as under:

Article 17.1 - Any dispute or claim arising out of or relating to this Agreement shall be in the first instance, endeavour to be settled amicably by negotiation between the parties hereto and failing which the same will be settled by arbitration pursuant to the English Arbitration Law and subsequent amendments thereto.

Article 17.2 - The arbitration proceedings shall be carried out by two Arbitrators one appointed by BALCO and one by KATSI chosen freely and without any bias. The court of Arbitration shall be held wholly in London, England and shall use English language in the proceeding. The findings and award of the Court of Arbitration shall be final and binding upon the parties.

Article 22 - Governing Law - This agreement will be governed by the prevailing law of India and in case of Arbitration, the English law shall apply.[3]

4 . The aforesaid clause itself indicates that by reason of the agreement between the parties, the governing law of the agreement was the prevailing law of India. However, the settlement procedure for adjudication of rights or obligations under the agreement was by way of arbitration in London and the English Arbitration Law was made applicable to such proceedings. Therefore, the *lex fori* for the arbitration is English Law but the substantive law will be Indian Law.[4]

5. Disputes arose between the parties with regard to the performance of the agreement. Claim was made by the Appellant for return of its investment in the modernization programme, loss, profits and other sums. The Respondent made a claim for unclaimed instalments plus interest and damages for breach of intellectual property rights. Negotiations to reach a settlement of the disputes between the parties were unsuccessful and a written notice of request for arbitration was issued by the Respondent to the Appellant by a notice dated 13th November, 1997. The disputes were duly referred to arbitration which was held in England. The arbitral tribunal made two awards dated 10th November, 2002 and 12th November, 2002 in England. The Appellant thereafter filed applications Under Section 34 of the Arbitration Act, 1996 for setting aside the aforesaid two awards in the Court of the learned District Judge, Bilaspur which were numbered as MJC Nos. 92 of 2003 and 14 of 2003, respectively. By an order dated 20th July, 2004, the learned District Judge, Bilaspur held that the applications filed by the Appellant Under Section 34 of the Arbitration and Conciliation Act, 1996 (hereinafter referred to as the 'Arbitration Act, 1996') for setting aside the foreign awards are not tenable and accordingly dismissed the same.[5]

6. Aggrieved by the aforesaid judgment, the Appellant filed two miscellaneous appeals being Misc. Appeal Nos. 889 of 2004 and Misc. Appeal No. 890 of 2004 in the High Court of Judicature at Chattisgarh, Bilaspur. By an order dated 10th August, 2005, a Division Bench of the High Court dismissed the appeal. It was held as follows:

For the aforesaid reasons, we hold that the applications filed by the Appellant Under Section 34 of the Indian Act are not maintainable against the two foreign awards dated 10.11.2002 and 12.11.2002 and accordingly dismiss Misc. Appeal No. 889 of 2004 and Misc. Appeal No. 890 of 2004, but order that the parties shall bear their own costs.

The aforesaid decision has been challenged in this appeal.[6]

Held, while allowing the appeal

1. In view of the above discussion, we are of the considered opinion that the Arbitration Act, 1996 has accepted the territoriality principle which has been adopted in the UNCITRAL Model Law. Section 2(2) makes a declaration that Part I of the Arbitration Act, 1996 shall apply to all arbitrations which take place within India. We are of the considered opinion that Part I of the Arbitration Act, 1996 would have no application to International Commercial Arbitration held outside India. Therefore, such awards would only be subject to the jurisdiction of the Indian courts when the same are sought to be enforced in India in accordance with the provisions contained in Part II of the Arbitration Act, 1996. In our opinion, the provisions contained in Arbitration Act, 1996 make it crystal clear that there can be no overlapping or intermingling of the provisions contained in Part I with the provisions contained in Part II of the Arbitration Act, 1996.[197]

2. With utmost respect, we are unable to agree with the conclusions recorded in the judgments of this Court in Bhatia International (supra) and Venture Global Engineering (supra). In our opinion, the provision contained in Section 2(2) of the Arbitration Act, 1996 is not in conflict

with any of the provisions either in Part I or in Part II of the Arbitration Act, 1996. In a foreign seated international commercial arbitration, no application for interim relief would be maintainable under Section 9 or any other provision, as applicability of Part I of the Arbitration Act, 1996 is limited to all arbitrations which take place in India. Similarly, no suit for interim injunction simplicitor would be maintainable in India, on the basis of an international commercial arbitration with a seat outside India.[198]

3. We conclude that Part I of the Arbitration Act, 1996 is applicable only to all the arbitrations which take place within the territory of India.[199]

4. The judgment in Bhatia International (supra) was rendered by this Court on 13th March, 2002. Since then, the aforesaid judgment has been followed by all the High Courts as well as by this Court on numerous occasions. In fact, the judgment in Venture Global Engineering (supra) has been rendered on 10th January, 2008 in terms of the ratio of the decision in Bhatia International (supra). Thus, in order to do complete justice, we hereby order, that the law now declared by this Court shall apply prospectively, to all the arbitration agreements executed hereafter.[200]

• • •

CHAPTER XV

Ramesh Chand vs. Asruddin and Ors. (06.10.2015 – SC) : MANU/SC/1099/2015

Relative Section: Specific Relief Act 1963 - Section 20, Specific Relief Act 1963 - Section 20(2)

Hon'ble Judges/Coram: Dipak Misra and Prafulla C. Pant, JJ.

Equivalent Citation: 2015(156)AIC270, 2016(4)ALLMR492, 2016 (115) ALR 21, 2015(4)BLJ180, 2015 (6)BomCR243, (2016)2CALLT40(SC), 2015(4)CDR881(SC), 2016(1) CHN (SC) 26, 121(2016)CLT269, 2015 (II)CLR(SC)1033, 2015/INSC/735, 2015(4)J.L.J.R.218, 2016-2-LW558, 2016(4)MhLj15, (2015) 7MLJ 503 (SC),2016(3)MPLJ77, 2016(I)OLR169, 2015(4)PLJR346, 2015(4)RCR(Civil)719, 2016 131 RD267, 2015 (10) SCALE433, (2016)1SCC653, 2016 (2) SCJ 3, [2015]10SCR604, 2015 (4) WLN 111 (SC)

Number of Pages in the Original Judgment: 5

Case Reference: nil

Case Note:

Contract - Specific Performance of Contract - Plaintiff/ Respondent No. 1 entered into agreement - Appellant agreed to sell land - Agreement for sale executed - Further agreed - Land in suit, mortagaged with Defendant No. 2 - Be redeemed by the Appellant before execution - Notice to Appellant to execute sale deed - Failure - Suit for specific performance of contract - Trial court disposed suit - Held - Not a fit case for specific performance - Directed to pay back earnest money - Plaintiff filed civil appeal - First appellate court allowed appeal - Decreed suit for specific performance - Regular second appeal filed - Dismissed upholding order of first appellant - Appeal through special leave - Whether High Court was justified in upholding the order of first appellate court decreeing the suit for specific performance of contract

Facts:

Plaintiff/ Respondent No. 1 entered into an agreement with Defendant No. 1/ Appellant Ramesh Chand whereby the Appellant agreed to sell his land to the Respondent No. 1. An agreement for sale was executed between the parties after the Appellant accepted some amount as a part of consideration. It was further agreed between the parties that the land in suit, mortgaged with Defendant No. 2/ Respondent No. 2 Gurgaon Gramin Bank, Nagina, would be redeemed by the Appellant before execution of the sale deed. The Plaintiff/Respondent No. 1 gave notice to the Appellant to execute the sale deed and remained present with the balance amount of consideration in the Office of Sub Registrar, Nagina, and got his presence marked. But the Appellant failed to turn up to execute the sale deed, as agreed between him and the Respondent No. 1. Hence the suit for specific performance of contract was filed.

After recording oral testimony of witnesses of the parties, and considering the documentary evidence on record, the trial court came to the conclusion that it is not a fit case for specific performance of contract, and disposed of the suit with a finding that the agreement executed between the Plaintiff and Defendant No. 1 was in substance an agreement of security for repayment of loan and directed the Defendant No. 1 to pay back earnest money of rupees four lacs with 8% interest per annum from 21.06.2004 till payment is made to the Plaintiff. Aggrieved, Plaintiff filed Civil Appeal before first Appellate Court. The Appellate Court allowed the appeal and decreed the suit for specific performance of contract, directing Defendant No. 1 to execute the sale deed in terms of the agreement after accepting balance amount from the Plaintiff. This made Defendant No. 1 Ramesh Chand to file Regular Second Appeal before the High Court. During the Second Appeal, Defendant No. 1 appears to have died, and his legal heirs prosecuted the appeal. After hearing the parties, the High Court dismissed the appeal upholding the order passed by the first appellate court. Hence this appeal before us through special leave.

Held, while disposing the appeal

It is pertinent to mention here that in the present case, though execution of agreement dated 21.06.2004 between the parties is proved, but it is no where pleaded or proved by the Plaintiff that he got redeemed the mortgaged land in favour of Defendant No. 2 in terms of the agreement, nor is it specifically pleaded that he was ready and willing to get the property redeemed from the mortgage.[8]

In the above facts and circumstances of the case and the judicial principle discussed above, we are of the opinion that it is a fit case where instead of granting decree of specific performance, the Plaintiff can be compensated by directing the Appellant to pay a reasonable and sufficient amount to him. We are of the view that mere refund of rupees four lacs with interest at the rate of 8% per annum, as directed by the trial court, would be highly insufficient. In our considered opinion, it would be just and appropriate to direct the Appellants (Legal Representatives of original Defendant No. 1, since died) to repay rupees four lacs along with interest at the rate of 18% per annum from 21.06.2004 till date within a period of three months from today to the L. Rs. of Respondent No. 1. If they do so, the decree of specific performance shall stand set aside. We clarify that if the amount is not paid or deposited before the trial court in favour of the L. Rs. of Respondent No. 1 within a period of three months, as directed above, the decree of specific performance shall stand affirmed. We order accordingly.[9]

• • •

CHAPTER XVI

Hanumappa Channappa Hullur vs. Shivamaruthappa Parappa Kalli and Ors. (21.08.2015 – SC) : MANU/SC/0906/2015

Relative Section:

Specific Relief Act, 1877 - Section 14, Section 15, Section 16, Section 17; Specific Relief Act 1963 - Section 12, Section 12(2), Section 12(3), Section 15

Hon'ble Judges/Coram:

M.Y. Eqbal and C. Nagappan, JJ.

Equivalent Citation:

2016 (115) ALR 140, 2015 5 AWC4523SC, 2015(3)CLJ(SC)121, 2015(II)CLR(SC)707, 2015/INSC/592, 2015 (4) RCR(Civil)203, 2016 131 RD373, 2015(9)SCALE328, [2015]9SCR798, (2016)4WBLR(SC)58

Number of Pages in the Original Judgment: 7

Case Reference:

Jenkins v. Hiles 6 Ves. 646; Mortlock v. Duller 10 Ves. 315; Rathorgford v. Acton Adams MANU/PR/ 0115/1915 : AIR 1915 PC 113; A. Abdul Rashid Khan (Dead) and Ors. v. P.A.K.A. Shahul Hamid and Ors. MANU/ SC/2734/2000 : (2000) 10 SCC 636; Kammana Sambamurthy (Dead) by L.Rs. v. Kalipatnapu Atchutamma (Dead) and Ors. MANU/SC/0809/2010 : (2011) 11 SCC 153; HPA International v. Bhagwandas Fateh Chand Daswani and Ors. MANU/SC/0536/2004 : (2004) 6 SCC 537; Kartar Singh v. Harjinder Singh MANU/SC/0158/1990 : (1990) 3 SCC 517

Case Note:

Civil - Sale of property - Section 12 of the Specific Relief Act, 1963 - Appellant purchased property from Respondent No. 1 who represented himself as owner of whole - Appellant paid over 50% of sale price of property - Respondents refused to execute sale deed - Respondent Nos. 2 and 3 claimed share in property - Contract to sell could not be performed - High Court dismissed Appellant's suit for specific performance - Whether the High Court was justified in dismissing the Appellant's suit for specific performance of a partial suit

Contract - Partial performance - Specific Relief Act, 1963 - Respondent No. 1 had share only in 1/3rd of property - Whether Appellant is entitled to specific performance of contract to sell in respect of the whole property - Whether partial performance can be ordered against the Respondents

Facts

The Appellant agreed to purchase land from Respondent No. 1, who claimed the property to be self-acquired and was selling it for legal necessity, for Rs. 72,000. A sum of Rs. 53,000/- as earnest money was paid by the Appellant and received by Respondent No. 1. An agreement was signed and on the same day Respondent No. 1 delivered possession of the land to Appellant, who has been in possession since. Respondent No. 1 failed to receive balance consideration amount of Rs. 19,000 and execute sale deed as agreed earlier, upon which the Appellant gave notice to perform their part of contract, since the he was ready and willing to perform his part of contract.

The Appellant filed a seeking specific performance of a contract between him and Respondent No. 1 for sale of land, and restraining the Respondents from interfering in his possession of the land. Conversely, Respondent Nos. 2 and 3 (sons of Respondent No. 1) filed a suit against the Appellant for a declaration that the agreement to sell land by Respondent No. 1 was not binding on them and their share in the land, and to grant permanent injunction restraining the Appellant from interfering in their possession of the land. The Respondent's suit was dismissed by the trial court, its decision upheld on appeal. At the High Court, the Respondent's appeal was allowed while the Appellant's suit was dismissed. Hence, the present appeal.

Held,

1.In a case where the seller had held himself as the owner of the whole, the case would have been different, but in the absence of misrepresentation or misconduct, the general rule is that where a person is jointly interested in an estate with another person and purports to deal with the entirety, specific performance will not be granted against him as to his share. The departure from the Act, 1877 in the Act, 1963 is that under the Act, 1877 the party seeking specific performance had to pay the entire amount of consideration stipulated in the agreement even where it was seeking enforcement of a part of a contract, but under Act, 1963 it has to pay only a part of consideration after abatement in the amount of consideration.[2] and[7]

2.The High Court was correct in holding that the agreement entered into by Respondent No. 1 without the concurrence of the other sharers namely Respondent Nos. 2 and 3 to sell the joint family property is not legal and valid. The terms of the sale agreement show that Respondent No. 1 represented to the Appellant that he was the absolute owner of the property It confirmed that the Appellant is in possession of the property. Therefore, this is not a case which is covered by Section 12 of the Act.[19],[20] and[22]

3.The Court in Abdul Rashid Khan (Dead) and Ors. v. P.A.K.A. Shahul Hamid and Ors. held: "in the absence of the other co-sharer, there could not be any decree of any specified part of the property to be partitioned and possession given. The decree could only be to the extent of transferring the share of the Appellants in such property to other such contracting party." In Kammana Sambamurthy (Dead) by L.Rs. v. Kalipatnapu Atchutamma (Dead) and Ors. it was added that the buyer is not entitled to seek specific performance of the agreement to the extent of half share of the seller's wife (who did not sell) and there is no impediment for enforcement of the agreement against the seller to the extent of his half share in the property. Based on this rationale, there is no impediment for enforcement of the sale agreement against Respondent No. 1 to the extent of his $1/3^{rd}$ share in the suit property.[23],[24] and[25]

• • •

CHAPTER XVII

Satya Pal Anand vs. State of M.P. and Ors. (25.08.2015 – SC) : MANU/SC/0925/2015

Relative Section:

Madhya Pradesh Co-operative Societies Act, 1960 - Section 57(1), Madhya Pradesh Co-operative Societies Act, 1960 - Section 64, Madhya Pradesh Co-operative Societies Act, 1960 - Section 69;

Registration Act, 1908 - Section 16A(1), Section 17, Section 17(1), Section 18, Section 19,Section 20, Section 21, Section 21(1), Section 21(2), Section 21(3), Section 22, Section 22A, Section 25, Section 31, Section 32, Section 32A,Section 33, Section 34, Section 34A, Section 35, Section 51, Section 63, Section 69,Section 88, Section 88(2), Section 89;

Transfer of Property Act, 1882 - Section 54;

Indian Contract Act, 1872 - Section 62;

Specific Relief Act 1963 - Section 31, Section 31(1),Section 31(2);

Karnataka Stamp Act, 1957;

Income Tax Act, 1961 - Section 230A, Income Tax Act, 1961 - Section 269UL;

Urban Land (Ceiling and Regulation) Act, 1976 [Repealed] - Section 26;

Limitation Act, 1963 - Schedule - Article 59;

Agricultural Marketing Act, 1958; Andhra Pradesh Registration Rules - Rule 26, Andhra Pradesh Registration Rules - Rule 58, Andhra Pradesh Registration Rules - Rule 69, Andhra Pradesh Registration Rules - Rule 117; Madhya Pradesh Cooperative Societies Rules, 1962;

Constitution of India - Article 12, Article 32, Article 136, Article 226, Article 300A

Hon'ble Judges/Coram: Dipak Misra and V. Gopala Gowda, JJ.

Equivalent Citation: 2015(155)AIC129, 2015 (113) ALR 284, 2016ALT (Rev.) 44, 2015 (5) AWC 5273 (SC), 2015(4) CDR820 (SC),2015/INSC/603, 2016 130 RD256, 2015(9)SCALE297, (2015)15SCC263, 2015 (9) SCJ 538, [2015] 14SCR92

Number of Pages in the Original Judgment: 27

Case Reference:

Yanala Malleshwari v. Anantula Sayamma MANU/AP/0747/2006 : AIR 2007 AP 57; E.R. Kalaivan v. Inspector General of Registration, Chennai and Anr. MANU/TN/1864/2009 : AIR 2010 Madras 18; G.D. Subramaniam v. The Sub-Registrar, Konur MANU/TN/0600/2009 : 2009 CIJ 243 Madras; M. Ramakrishna Reddy v. Sub Registrar, Bangalore and Anr. MANU/KA/0692/1999 : AIR 2000 Karnataka 46; Thota Ganga Laxmi and Anr. v. Government of Andhra Pradesh and Ors. MANU/SC/1267/2010 : (2010) 15 SCC 207; Park View Enterprises v. State of Tamil Nadu MANU/TN/0100/1989 : AIR 1990 Mad 251; Satya Pal Anand v. Punjabi Housing Cooperative Society and Ors. SLP (C) No. 13255 of 2012; Government of U.P. v. Raja Mohammad Amir Ahmad Khan MANU/SC/0030/1961 : AIR 1961 SC 787; City Bank N.A. v. Standard Chartered Bank and Ors. MANU/SC/0793/2003 : 2004 (1) SCC 12; Pratap Singh v. State of Punjab MANU/SC/0272/1963 : AIR 1964 SC 72; Municipal Council of Sydney v. Campbell; Marquess of Clanricarde v. Congested Districts Board; Short v. Poole Corporation Pollock M.R.; Reg. v. Governors of Darlington School; Arunachalam v. P.S.R. Sadhanantham and Anr. MANU/SC/0073/1979 : (1979) 2 SCC 297; Ganga Kumar Shrivastav v. State of Bihar MANU/SC/0420/2005 : (2005) 6 SCC 211; CAG v. K.S. Jagannathan MANU/SC/0066/1986 : (1986) 2 SCC 679; Mayor of Rochester v. Regina; King v. Revising Barrister for the Borough of Hanley; Padfield v. Minister of Agriculture, Fisheries and Food; Andi Mukta Sadguru Shree Muktajee Vandas Swami Suvarna Jayanti Mahotsav Smarak Trust v. V.R. Rudani MANU/SC/0028/1989 : (1989) 2 SCC 691; Praga Tools Corporation v. C.A. Imanual; Hari Vishnu Kamath v. Ahmad Ishaque MANU/SC/0095/1954 : AIR 1955 SC 233

Case Note:

Property - Cancellation of registered documents - Section 17 Registration Act, 1908 and Madhya Pradesh Cooperative Societies Rules, 1962 - Appellant's mother allotted land by Respondent No. 4 - Did not construct house for over 35 years - Respondent No. 4 unilaterally cancelled allotment after death of Appellant's mother and executed deed of extinguishment - Entered into sale deed with Respondent No. 5 - Respondent No. 5 entered into further sale deed - Appellant filed application before Respondent No. 3 for cancellation of registered deeds - Application rejected for lack of jurisdiction - Petitions before High Court rejected - Dispute was to be adjudicated before appropriate authority - Whether in the absence of any specific rule in the Rules the general principle laid down in the case of Thota Ganga Laxmi and Anr. v. Government of Andhra Pradesh and Ors. would be applicable - Whether the Deed of Extinguishment and the subsequent sale deeds registered by Resp. No. 3 could be cancelled by him or his superior authority in exercise of powers under Sec. 17 Act, 1908

Civil - Discretionary power - Article 226 Constitution of India, 1950 - High Court refused to adjudicate Appellant's petition for cancellation of registered deeds - Jurisdiction to determine issue lay with appropriate adjudicatory authority - Whether Respondent No. 3 had undertaken a role in the nature of public duty - Whether on the facts the High Court erred in not issuing a writ

Facts

The Appellant filed an application dated 4.2.2008 in the office of the Sub-Registrar, Respondent No. 3, for cancellation of registered documents dated 9.8.2001, 21.4.2004 and 11.7.2006 which pertain to registration of immovable property. According to the application, the plot was allotted to his mother by Respondent No. 4, by entering into a sale deed dated 22.3.1962, registered on 30.03.1962. After death of the Appellant's mother on 12.6.1988, Respondent No. 4, through its office bearer executed a Deed of Extinguishment on 9.8.2001 unilaterally cancelling the said allotment and on the strength of such document, executed a registered sale deed dated 21.4.2004 in favour of Respondent No. 5, who in turn executed another sale deed dated 11.7.2006 in favour of the Respondent Nos. 6 and 7.

Respondent No. 3 rejected the application for two reasons: dispute between the parties was pending before the competent authority; and his jurisdiction was limited only to the extent of registering the documents, if any party desired cancellation, then to verify that the cancellation deed was registered on appropriate stamp paper. The Appellant filed an application under Section 69 of the Registration Act, 1908 which was rejected by the Inspector General (Registration) stating that the powers conferred on it were limited to general superintendence of the registration office and making rules and not to provide hearing by any Sub-Registrar.

The High Court held that the controversy raised by the Appellant could be adjudicated before the appropriate forum and not in the writ proceeding. The High Court further held that the authorities under the Act had correctly stated that they have no jurisdiction to decide the soundness of registration of Extinguishment Deed or the sale deeds and declare them null and void. Hence, the present appeal.

Held,

1.Dipak Misra, J. delivered the following opinion. In Yanala Malleshwari v. Anantula Sayamma, it was held: "The person, who has ex facie right whether such right is registered or not can always approach the registering authority, with a request to cancel a sale deed, which was registered earlier by such registering authority", "...there is no specific prohibition under the Registration Act, 1908 to register a deed of cancellation...it is not in dispute that the cancellation deed fulfills the conditions for the purpose of registration. However, the Act does not permit the Registering Officer to enquire into the title of the party presenting the document for registration and the situations mentioned in the above said provisions under which the registration can be refused are for different purpose and only under those contingencies he can refuse." By the decision in Yanala Malleshwari v. Anantula Sayamma, if a person is aggrieved by the cancellation deed, his remedy is to seek an appropriate relief in the civil court and the writ petition is not the proper remedy. There is no prohibition to register a document of cancellation or deed of extinguishment. Section 35 of the Act, 1908 cannot be construed to confer a quasi-judicial power on the registering authority.[15] and[24]

2.In the absence of any power conferred on the Registering Authority to adjudicate any aspect, the decision in Thota Ganga Laxmi and Anr. v. Government of Andhra Pradesh and Ors. that the Registering Authority cannot unilaterally register a deed of cancellation, cannot be agreed with. In the absence of any rule which commands the Registering Officer to ensure at the time of preparation for registration of cancellation deeds of previously registered deed of conveyances on sale before him that such cancellation deeds are executed by all the executant and claimant parties to the previously registered conveyance on sale and that such cancellation deed is accompanied by declaration showing natural consent, the Registering Authority or the superior authority cannot refuse to register a deed of cancellation solely on the ground that the claimant parties to the previously registered conveyance are not present or they have not given consent.[25]

3.Under Section 69 of the Act, 1908 the Inspector General is empowered to make rules consistent with the Act, 1908. The Rules provide the manner of verification of execution. It is a condition precedent for the purpose of execution and registration. In the absence of any rule to opine that by no stretch of imagination can a cancellation deed be accepted or registered by the Registering Authority does not appear to be correct. No error in the dismissal of the petition by the High Court is found. The principle stated in Thota Ganga Laxmi and Anr. v. Government of Andhra Pradesh and Ors. requires consideration by a larger bench.[26] and[30]

4.V. Gopala Gowda, J. dissented. The documents filed by the Respondents have been fraudulently registered by them which are against the acquired legal rights of the Appellant on the said plot of land. The same are void ab initio in law as it is impermissible under the provisions of the Indian Registration Act, 1908 read with Section 31 of the Specific Relief Act, 1963. Respondent No. 4 has no right to re-allot the said plot of land in favour of the Respondent No. 5 by cancelling the already registered sale deed in favour of the Appellant's mother. Registering of sale deed in favour of Respondent No. 5, who in turn sold the said plot of land in favour of Respondent Nos. 6 and 7, is void ab initio as in the bye-laws of Respondent No. 4, Respondent No. 5 could not have come in possession of the said plot. Therefore, the transfer of the said plot of land via subsequent sale deeds are void ab initio in law as well.[38] and[50]

5.The extinguishment deed, which is unilaterally registered would be rescinded in the case of sale deed or extinguishment deed. Thus, Section 62 of the Indian Contract Act, 1872 would provide that if the parties to a contract agree to substitute a new contract for it, or to rescind or alter it, the original contract need not be performed. For any novation, rescission and alteration of the contract, it can be made only bilaterally and with the amicable consent of both the parties. A deed of cancellation of the earlier registered sale deed executed in favour of the Appellant's mother would amount to an illegal rescission of the absolute sale deed because if the issue in question is viewed from the application of Section 62 of the Indian Contract Act, 1872, any rescission must be done only bilaterally. Further, the unilateral cancellation of the sale deed with regard to the land against the Appellant is contrary to the provisions as provided under Section 31 of the Specific Relief Act, 1963 read with Article 59 of the Limitation Act, 1963, wherein the cancellation of any instrument can be done only within three years, 'when the facts entitling the Plaintiff to have the instrument or decree cancelled or set aside or the contract rescinded first become known to him'. The registration of the document by Respondent No. 3 amounts to playing fraud on the power provided to him under law which is ultra vires the relevant statutory provisions and the Constitution of India.[47] and[49]

6.In CAG v. K.S. Jagannathan, it was held "Even had the Division Bench issued a writ of mandamus giving the directions which it did, if circumstances of the case justified such directions, the High Court would have been entitled in law to do so... writ in the nature of mandamus or to pass orders and give necessary directions where the government or a public authority has failed to exercise or has wrongly exercised the discretion conferred upon it by a statute or a rule or a policy decision of the government or has exercised such discretion mala fide or on irrelevant considerations or by ignoring the relevant considerations and materials or in such a manner as to frustrate the object of conferring such discretion or the policy for implementing which such discretion has been conferred. In all such cases and in any other fit and proper case a High Court can, in the exercise of its jurisdiction Under Article 226, issue a writ of mandamus or a writ in the nature of mandamus or pass orders and give directions to compel the performance in a proper and lawful manner of the discretion conferred upon the government or a public authority, and in a proper case, in order to prevent injustice resulting to the concerned parties, the court may itself pass an order or give directions which the government or the public authority should have passed or given had it properly and lawfully exercised its discretion." In Andi Mukta Sadguru Shree Muktajee Vandas Swami Suvarna Jayanti Mahotsav Smarak Trust v. V.R. Rudani, "The words "any person or authority" used in Article 226 are, therefore, not to be confined only to statutory authorities and instrumentalities of the State. They may cover any other person or body performing public duty. The form of the body concerned is not very much relevant. What is relevant is the nature of the duty imposed on the body. The duty must be judged in the light of positive obligation owed by the person or authority to the affected party. No matter by what means the duty is imposed, if a positive obligation exists mandamus cannot be denied....Here again we may point out that mandamus cannot be denied on the ground that the duty to be enforced is not imposed by the statute."[55] and[56]

7. In Hari Vishnu Kamath v. Ahmad Ishaque, the Court had mentioned several instances where Certiorari could be issued in a broad set of circumstances, such as when there was an error in decision or judgment of an inferior court and was in the disregard of the provisions of the law. Thus, the High Court failed to exercise its discretionary power.[57] and[58]

● ● ●

CHAPTER XVIII

Shamsher Singh and Ors. vs. Rajinder Kumar and Ors. (16.04.2014 – SC) : MANU/SC/0333/2014

Relative Section: Specific Relief Act 1963 - Section 13, Section 20(2), Section 21(2)

Hon'ble Judges/Coram: S.J. Mukhopadhaya and V. Gopala Gowda, JJ.

Equivalent Citation: 2014v AD (S.C.) 117, 2014(138)AIC68, AIR2014SC2253, 2014(5)ALD95(SC), 2014 (104) ALR 905, 2014 (4) AWC 3274 (SC), (SCSuppl)2015(4)CHN151, 2015(4)CTC441, 2014(I) CLR (SC) 1158, 2014/INSC/283, JT2014(5)SC319, 2014(2)RCR(Civil)865, 2014 124 RD293, 2014(5)SCALE292, (2015)5SCC531, 2016 (1) SCJ 35, (2015)1WBLR(SC)390

Number of Pages in the Original Judgment: 6

Case Reference:

A.C. Arulappan v. Ahalya Naik MANU/SC/0438/2001 : (2001) 6 SCC 600

Case Note:

Suit - For specific performance against appellants alleging that agreement to sell entered with respect to suit land--Defendants filed written statement contending in that they had never entered into any agreement to sell suit land to plaintiffs--Inequitable to grant decree of specific performance where it is clear that plaintiffs have unfair advantage over defendants--Extremely likely that plaintiff tried to take unfair advantage of defendants--Trial court rightly exercised its discretion not to grant specific performance--Trial court's judgment not to decree specific performance of purported agreement of sale--Upheld--Impugned judgment and order of High Court--Set aside.

Facts:

The factual matrix of the case is as follows:

The Respondents (original Plaintiffs) filed a suit for specific performance against the Appellants herein alleging that an agreement to sell dated 3rd June, 2002 was entered between them with respect to the suit land. It was alleged that out of ` 3,00,000/- (total agreed consideration), ` 2,00,000/- had already been paid by the Plaintiffs on 3rd June, 2002 and as per agreement, the balance amount were to be paid at the time of execution of sale deed, i.e. on 20th December, 2002. It was further alleged that later, the Defendant-Appellants became dishonest and wanted to sell the land to some other persons. Therefore, they had to file the suit.

Held, while allowing the appeal

Further we find it necessary to refer to Para 3 of the pleadings wherein it is stated as under:

3. That the Defendants No. 1 to 3 entered into an agreement to sell the suit land as detailed and described in the head note of the plaint with Plaintiffs for a sum of ` 3,00,000/- (Rs. Three Lacs) and they executed agreement to sell dated 3.6.2002 and received earnest money of ` 2,00,000/- (Rs. Two Lacs) and executed a valid receipt on the foot of the agreement to sell dated 3.6.2002 in the presence of witnesses.

This receipt has been executed on the same day, i.e. on 3-6-2002 as the agreement of sale, and the terms of the receipt are in direct contradiction with the terms of the agreement, as the receipt says that ` 2,00,000/- has been received by the Defendant Nos. 1 to 3 whereas the agreement of sale speaks only of ` 1,00,000/- that has changed hands and the Plaintiff will pay the Defendant Nos. 1 to 3 the remaining ` 2,00,000/- at the time of registration. Further, in the written statement, the Defendants have pleaded that they only took a loan of ` 85,000 and mortgaged their land as security and were tricked into putting their thumb impressions on the purported agreement of sale.

It is clear from all this that the discrepancies make it difficult for us to accept that the Defendant Nos. 1 to 3 have intended for this to be an agreement of sale and it is extremely likely that the Plaintiff has tried to take unfair advantage of them. It is prudent on our part, therefore, to uphold the Trial Court's judgment not to decree specific performance of the purported agreement of sale. We will modify the Trial Court's decree insofar as the amount is concerned and order the Defendant Nos. 1 to 3 to return ` 2,00,000/- with interest and not an amount of ` 3,00,000/- as directed by the Trial Court.

Answer to point No. 2

13. Another important aspect of this case that has slipped the eyes of the courts below is the question of the mortgage of the suit property, as pleaded by the Defendant Nos. 4 and 5. They placed the confirmation of mutation in favour of the Bank, Ex. D-1 and the Mortgage deed, Ex. D-2 as evidence. The Plaintiffs have referred to the same in para 2 of their

pleadings and the Defendants, in reply have admitted this in para 2 of their written statement wherein they have stated that it is a matter of record that they have mortgaged their portion of the land in favour of Defendant Nos. 4 and 5. More importantly, the Plaintiffs have admitted the same in para 2 of their plaint, therefore it was in their knowledge that the land in question was already mortgaged with Defendant Nos. 4 and 5. There has been no finding recorded on the same by either the appellate courts or the Trial Court and as per Section 13(c) of the Act, when the vendor (the Defendants herein) professes to sell unencumbered property but the same is mortgaged, then the vendor has only a right to redeem it and the purchaser may compel him to redeem the mortgage and to obtain a valid discharge. This aspect of the matter, too, has not been dealt with by the Trial Court or the appellate courts.

Answer to point No. 3

14. Thus, the judgment and order of the Trial Court must be modified and the judgments and orders of the appellate courts must be reversed. There are many discrepancies on the face of this case and the Trial Court would have done well to examine all the evidence with care and diligence, which has not been done in the present case. In spite of the same, it would be prudent to uphold the judgment and decree of the Trial Court by modifying it instead of the judgments and orders of the appellate courts which have decreed the original suit for specific performance of the agreement to sell the suit schedule property.

15. For the foregoing reasons, these appeals are allowed, the impugned judgment and order passed by the High Court is set aside and the judgment and decree passed by the Trial Court in Civil Suit No. 755 of 2003 is modified in the aforesaid terms. We thereby, order and direct the Defendant Nos. 1 to 3 to repay the Plaintiff an amount of ` 2,00,000/- with interest @6% per annum within six weeks from the date of receipt of the certified copy of this judgment.

• • •

CHAPTER XIX

Inderchand Jain (D) through L.Rs. vs. Motilal (D) through L.Rs. (21.07.2009 – SC) : MANU/SC/1297/2009

Relative Section:

Code of Civil Procedure, 1908 (CPC) - Section 113; Code of Civil Procedure, 1908 (CPC) - Section 114; Specific Relief Act 1963 - Section 16(c), Specific Relief Act 1963 - Section 20, Specific Relief Act 1963 - Section 20(2)(b)

Hon'ble Judges/Coram: S.B. Sinha and Deepak Verma, JJ.

Equivalent Citation:

2009(81)AIC154, 2009 (76) ALR 782, 2009(7)ALT49(SC), 2009(2)ARC671, 2010 (2) AWC 1651 (SC), 2009 (3) CCC 365,2009(5)CTC365, JT2009(9)SC537, (2009)8MLJ743(SC), 2009(9)SCALE777,(2009)14 SCC 663, [2009]11SCR252

Number of Pages in the Original Judgment: 11

Case Reference:

Rajendra Kumar v. Rambai MANU/SC/0542/2002; Lily Thomas v. Union of India MANU/SC/0327/2000 ; Umabai and Anr. v. Nilkanth Dhondiba Chavan (Dead) By LRs. and Anr. MANU/SC/0285/2005; Sita Ram and Ors. v. Radhey Shyam MANU/SC/7988/2007; Ardeshir H. Mam v. Flora Sassoon MANU/MH/0116/1928 ; Board of Control for Cricket in India and Anr. v. Netaji Cricket Club and Ors. MANU/SC/0019/2005; Rajesh D. Darbar and Ors. v. Narasingrao Krishnaji Kulkarni and Ors. MANU/SC/0544/2003; Jagmohan Singh v. State of Punjab and Ors. MANU/SC/7541/2008

Case Note:

Civil-Review -Jurisdiction -Present appeal is filed to challenge impugned judgment of high court passed in revision petition which gave rise to question of jurisdiction of a Court and extent thereof to review its own decision - To what extent a Court is permitted to review its own decision - Held, application for review would be maintainable upon discovery of a new and important piece of evidence - When there exists an error apparent on face of record - If review is necessitated on account of some mistake or for any other sufficient reason - Any mistake on part of court which would include a mistake in nature of undertaking may also call for a review of order -What would constitute sufficient reason would depend on facts and circumstances of case - In present case, there were no sufficient ground to sustain valid review -Impugned judgment is set aside - Appeal allowed. [26]

Facts:

1. Before adverting to the aforementioned question, we may notice the admitted facts.[3]

An agreement was entered into by and between the parties on or about 15.10.1972 whereby and whereunder Inder Chand Jain-appellant had agreed to sell a 'haveli' to Motilal - respondent for a consideration of Rs. 1,15,000/-, out of which a sum of Rs. 20,000/- was paid in advance.

Respondent filed a suit for specific performance before the District Judge, Jaipur City, in which a decree was passed on 11.11.1975. Being dissatisfied, the appellant filed Civil First Appeal before the High Court which was allowed on 12.03.1987 whereby the judgment and order of the trial court was set aside.

On an intra court appeal filed by the respondent, a Division Bench of the High Court by its order dated 26.10.2005 remanded the matter back to the learned Single Judge for deciding the appeal afresh.

By an order dated 11.08.2006, a learned Single Judge of the High Court allowed the appeal once again and set aside the judgment and decree of the trial court.

2. Both the parties filed review petitions before the learned Single Judge of the High Court under Order XLVII Rule 1 of the Code of Civil Procedure seeking review of the judgment dated 11.08.2006. By the impugned judgment and order the learned Single Judge while allowing both the review petitions recalled its earlier judgment and order dated 11.08.2006 and directed the appeal to be listed for rehearing.[4]

3. Thus, the appellant-defendant is before this Court. [5]

Held, while allowing the appeal

1. For the reasons aforementioned, the impugned judgment cannot be sustained which is set aside accordingly. The appeal is allowed. However, it would be open to the plaintiff - respondent to file an appropriate application for recovery of such amount or amounts which he might have expended towards renovation of the building, which may be considered on its own merits. The court shall furthermore determine the

amount of mesne profit which became payable to the appellant. It would be open to the court to adjust the amount payable by the plaintiff to the defendant and vice-versa. [27]

• • •

CHAPTER XX

I.T.C. Ltd. vs. Adarsh Co-operative Housing Soc. Ltd. (27.08.2012 – SC) : MANU/SC/0677/2012

Relative Section:

Code of Civil Procedure, 1908 (CPC) - Section 115; Code of Civil Procedure, 1908 (CPC) - Section 145; Constitution Of India - Article 277; Specific Relief Act 1963 - Section 6, Specific Relief Act 1963 - Section 6(2), Specific Relief Act 1963 - Section 6(3)

Hon'ble Judges/Coram:

P. Sathasivam and Ranjan Gogoi, JJ.

Equivalent Citation:

2012(118)AIC96, 2012(6)ALD139, 2012 (94) ALR 682, 2012 5 AWC5356SC, 2012(4)BLJ86, 2013(1)CDR91(SC), 2012GLH(3)270, JT2012(8)SC183, (2012)7MLJ62, 2012(4)RCR(Civil)291, 2013(4)RLW2977(SC), 2012(8)SCALE11, (2013)10SCC169

Number of Pages in the Original Judgment: 6

Case Reference:

Lallu Yashwant Singh (dead) by his L.Rs.. v. Rao Jagdish Singh and Ors. AIR 1968 SC 620; Krishna Ram Mahale (D) by L.Rs.. v. Mrs. Shobha Venkat Rao MANU/SC/0278/1989 : AIR 1989 SC 2097; Sanjay Kumar Pandey and Ors. v. Gulabahar Sheikh and Ors. SCC 2004 (4) 664

Case Note:

Property - Possession - Courts below held that possession of disputed property on relevant date was with Plaintiff-Respondent from which he was unlawfully dispossessed by Defendant-Petitioner - Hence, this Appeal - Whether, Plaintiff-Respondent was in possession of disputed property on relevant date - Held, Respondent was in possession of southern portion was possible conclusion that could be reasonably reached in view of what was disclosed by police report read with relevant revenue records - Lease deed purported to be executed by Executors, on basis of which Petitioner claimed to haveentered possession of share of land belonging to Executors of lease deed had not been proved by Petitioner - agreement on basis of which Petitioner claimed possession of entire land had also not been proved -Signatures of Executors and witnesses of leasedeed and agreement had not been proved as required by law - Petitioner on dates of filing of Suits, was not in possession of Suit property - In such situation, dispossession which Respondent claimed to have taken place in intervening night had to be understood to have been proved and established - Issues raised by Petitioner with regard to validity of Sale deed executed by Executors in favour of Respondent on account of pendency of Suit and validity of entries in revenue records were questions surrounding title and were not strictly relevant for deciding issue that was required to be decided in Suit in question namely, who was in possession of Suit property on relevant date - Hence, findings recorded by Courts below were essentially findings on question of fact which have been arrived at on basis of evidence and materials adduced by parties - Therefore, there was no reason whatsoever, to disturb said findings of Courts below and same were affirmed - Appeal dismissed.

Facts:

The facts in brief, may now be noticed:[3]

The Respondent - Plaintiff had filed suit No. 72 of 1989 in the court of Civil Judge, Agra, under Section 6 of the Specific Relief Act, 1963, (hereinafter referred to as 'the Act') praying for delivery of possession of the suit property from which the plaintiff claimed to have been illegally dispossessed by the defendant (petitioner herein) in the night intervening 19th/20th of November, 1988. According to the Plaintiff, the land comprised in Khasra No. 877, measuring 2 bighas 3 biswas located in Village Basai Mustaqi Tajganj, Agra was jointly owned by Murari Lal on the one hand and Jagdish Prasad, Ramesh Chand, Suresh Chand and Haresh Chand (hereinafter referred to as 'Jagdish and Ors..') on the other. According to the Plaintiff, by mutual consent, Murari Lal was in possession of his half share in northern part of the land whereas the half share of Jagdish and Ors. was in the southern portion. The Plaintiff has averred that it came into possession of the southern portion of the plot (hereinafter referred to as the Suit land) on 22.5.1985 and on 03.01.1986 Jagdish and Ors. had sold the same to the Plaintiff. On the basis of the aforesaid sale made by a registered deed, the revenue records were corrected and necessary entries were made showing the name of the Plaintiff against the share of Jagdish and Ors.. According to the Plaintiff, Jagdish and Ors. had entered into an agreement of sale of the same land with the Defendant, though the land stood transferred in the name of the Plaintiff and the revenue records corrected accordingly. In these circumstances, according to the Plaintiff, suit No. 238 of 1983 was filed by the Defendant against Jagdish & others for specific performance of the agreement to sell. Another Suit i.e. Suit No. 765 of 1984 was also filed by the Defendant against Jagdish and Ors. for an order of injunction restraining Jagdish and Ors. from raising any construction on the suit land and from transferring/ alienating the same. According to the plaintiff, as the property involved in both the suits had already been transferred to the Plaintiff, the Plaintiff was impleaded as a party in both the above suits. It was also averred by the plaintiff that as injunction prayed for by the Defendant, as the plaintiff, in Suit No. 765 of 1984 was refused and the appeal against such refusal was dismissed, in the intervening night of 19th/20th November, 1988, forcible possession of the suit land was taken by the Defendant which fact was brought to the notice of concerned police station on 20.11.1988 itself. According to the plaintiff, a proceeding under Section 145 C.P.C. was also initiated at the instance of the Plaintiff wherein an order of attachment of the disputed land, i.e. the suit land, was passed on 29.11.1988. However, as the Defendant continued to remain in possession of the suit land despite the order of attachment, Suit No. 72/1989 was instituted by the Plaintiff seeking the reliefs already noticed.

Held, while allowing the appeal

The discussion that have preceded leads us to conclude that the findings recorded by the learned Trial Court and affirmed by the revisional Court as well as by the High Court are essentially findings on question of fact which have been arrived at on the basis of the evidence and materials adduced by the parties. We, therefore, find no reason whatsoever, to disturb the said findings and the same are hereby affirmed. Consequently, we dismiss the appeal and affirm the decree passed by the learned Courts below.[12]

• • •

CHAPTER XXI

Ram Niwas (Dead) Through Lrs. vs. Bano and Ors. (01.08.2000 – SC): MANU/SC/0468/2000

Relative Section:

Specific Relief Act 1963 - Section 19, Specific Relief Act 1963 - Section 19(b), Specific Relief Act 1963 - Section 20(2); Transfer Of Property Act, 1882 - Section 3

Hon'ble Judges/Coram:

S.S.M. Quadri and Shivaraj V. Patil, JJ.

Equivalent Citation:

AIR2000SC2921, 2001 (43) ALR 389, 2001(1)ARC241, 2000 (3) CCC 229 , JT2000(8)SC340, 2001-1-LW859 ,(2001)1MLJ33(SC), 2000(II)OLR(SC)446, 2001(1)PLJR18, 2000(4)RCR(Civil)83, 2000(5)SCALE363, (2000)6SCC685, [2000]Supp2SCR39, 2000(2)UJ1360

Number of Pages in the Original Judgment: 5

Case Reference:

Daniels v. Davison (1809) 16 Ves. 249; Faki Ibrahim v. Faki Gulam Mohidin MANU/MH/0303/1920; Mahadeo v. S.B. Kesarkar MANU/MH/ 0064/1972; Trilok Chand v. J.B. Bettie & Co. MANU/WB/0537/1925 : AIR 1926 Cal 204; Parthasaradhi Iyer v. Subbaraya Gramani MANU/TN/0055/ 1923 : AIR 1924 Mad 67; Mummidi Reddi Papannagari Yella Reddy v. Salla Subbi Reddy & Ors. AIR AP 20

Case Note:

Contract - specific performance - Section 19 (b) of Specific Relief Act, 1963 - appellant instituted suit for specific performance of agreement to sell property which was purchased by respondents - respondents claimed property on ground of purchase made in bonafide interest and without knowledge of previous agreement - High Court decided in favour of defendant holding defendant's contention right - Court found High Court's decision erroneous as defendant would deemed to have notice of previous agreement under circumstances of case - Court did not decide on question whether appellant should be granted remedy of specific performance and referred matter back to High Court on that question.

Facts:

1. The appellant (referred to as 'the tenant') is the unsuccessful plaintiff in the suit giving rise to this appeal. He took on rent a shop situated at Katlara Bazar, Loharawali Gali, Merta City (for short, 'the suit shop') from its owner, respondent No. 5 (referred to as, 'the vendor') and on the material date he was paying rent of Rs. 35/-per month. On January 25,1978, he claims to have entered into an agreement with the vendor to purchase the suit shop (Ext. 1) for a sum of Rs. 9200/- and paid a sum of Rs. 3200/- in cash and undertook to pay remaining amount of Rs. 6000/- at the time of execution of sale deed. During the pendency of this appeal he died and the appellants were substituted as his legal representatives. The tenant and the vendor are said to be closely related - they are brothers as well as brothers-in-law. Respondent Nos. 1 to 4 (referred to as 'the purchasers') purchased the suit shop from the vendor on July 24, 1978 for a sum of Rs. 20,000/- under Exhibit 4. On October 12, 1978 the tenant filed the suit for specific performance of Ext. 1 against the vendor and the purchasers and their respective husbands - respondent Nos. 6 to 9. The purchasers contested the suit denying genuineness of Ext. 1 and taking the plea that they are bona fide purchasers of the suit shop for value without notice of Ext. 1. On the basis of the pleadings the trial court framed necessary issues. Issue Nos. 1 and 10 which are relevant to the present discussion read as follows:

1. Had the defendant No. 1 agreed to sell the disputed shop to the plaintiff on 25-1-78 on the conditions written in para 2 of the plaint and put the plaintiff in possession as owner after taking Rs. 3200/-in its lieu, and entrusted the tenancy deed (letter) written by him and his father, dated Baisakhi Sudi 9 Samvat 2029, to the plaintiff?

10. Have the defendants Nos. 2 to 5 purchased the disputed shop after paying full price and had they no knowledge of the alleged agreement to sell?

Held, while allowing the appeal

1. The Division Bench in agreement with the learned Single Judge took the view that the plaintiff is not entitled to the relief of specific performance of Ext. 1. As on the question of genuineness and validity of Ext. 1, we are remanding the case to the learned Single Judge. We do not propose to express any opinion on this point and leave it to be decided afresh with reference to the provisions of Section 20(2) of the Specific Relief Act by the learned Single Judge after recording finding on issue No. 1.[20]

2. For the above reasons we set aside the judgment and order of the Division Bench confirming the judgment of the learned Single Judge and

remand the case to the learned Single Judge for his decision on (i) issue No. 1 and (ii) whether the plaintiff is entitled to the discretionary relief of specific performance of a contract in the light of Section 20(2) of the Specific Relief Act in accordance with law. The appeal is accordingly allowed but in the circumstances of the case, we make no order as to costs.[21]

• • •

Adv. Jayprakash Somani's Videos On Law

Adv. Jayprakash Somani's Videos on Law on Youtube- 'jaysomani64' channel.

1) SLP in Supreme Court / Special Leave Petitions in the Supreme Court of India

2) Transfer of Civil & Criminal Cases by the Supreme Court of India / Transfer of Matrimonial Cases

3) Appellate Jurisdiction of the Supreme Court of India

4) Jurisdictions of the Supreme Court of India

5) Public Interest Litigation in the Supreme Court of India / PIL in Supreme Court

6) Article 32 Writ Petitions in the Supreme Court of India

7) Bail Matters Top 10 Supreme Court Cases

8) FIR Quashing in High Court & Supreme Court

9) Bail & Anticipatory Bail Matters in Supreme Court

10) Insolvency & Bankruptcy Matters in the Supreme Court

11) Insolvency & Bankruptcy Code 2016 Part 1

12) Insolvency & Bankruptcy Code 2016 Part 2

13) Insolvency & Bankruptcy Code 2016 Part 3

14) Corporate Liquidation Process

15) Supreme Court Rules & Procedures Webinar of 2.5 hour on Zoom

16) RDDBFI Act, 1993 (Introduction)

17) The Indian Contact Act 1872

18) Negotiable Instruments Act (Introduction)

19) How to avoid matrimonial disputes& some more videos

20) SEBI Matters in the Supreme Court

21) Matrimonial Matters: Supreme Court's 20 Case Laws

22) Consumer Matters Supreme Court's 20 Case Laws

23) Service Matters Supreme Court's 20 Case Laws

24) How to Search Lawyer for Your Matter

25) Property Matters Supreme Court's 20 Case Laws

26) Bail Matters: Supreme Court's 20 Case Laws

27) Supreme Court / High Court Vacation Benches

28) 69000 Teacher's Recruitment Matters of UP Government in the Supreme Court

29) Contempt of Court Matters in the Supreme Court

30) Advocate Act's Matters in the Supreme Court

31) Business Law Matters in the Supreme Court

32) Banking Matters in the Supreme Court

33) Labour Law Matters in the Supreme Court

34) Arbitration Matters in the Supreme Court

35) Careers in Law -Zoom Webinar by Adv. Jayprakash Somani

36) Civil Matters in the Supreme Court

37) Consumer Protection Act | Consumer Matters in the Supreme Court

38) Corporate Matters in the Supreme Court

39) Criminal Matters in the Supreme Court

40) Role of Respondent in the Supreme Court of India

41) Motor Vehicle Accident Matters in Supreme Court with case laws

42) Article 131 Original Suits in Supreme Court

43) PIL in Supreme Court/ Public Interest Litigations in the Supreme Court of India'

44) CAB Citizenship Amendment Bill is not Unconstitutional

45) Supreme Court of India Cases & Process – Marathi

46) Legal Services Export / Export of Legal Services

47) Transfer of Matrimonial Cases by the Supreme Court of India

48) Public Interest Litigation PIL

49) The Specific Relief Act (Introduction)

50) Corporate Insolvency Resolution Process CIRP

51) ABMM's Career 5 - Careers in Law

52) Transfer of cases by Supreme Court

53) Writ Petitions in High Court & Supreme Court of India

54) Supreme Court Jurisdictions - Appeals, SLP, Writ Petitions, Transfer, Original, Review, Curative

55) LEGAL INDIA TV Show: Cases Handled in Supreme Court

56) Corporate Liquidation Process

57) Legal Services Export / Export of Legal Services

58) Corporate Laws

59) Election Matters- Supreme Court's 20 Case Laws

60) Companies Act, 2013

62) Competition Act, 2002

63) Banking Matters - Supreme Court's 20 Case Laws

64) Election Matters in the Supreme Court

65) Armed Forces Tribunal Matters in the Supreme Court

66) Compassionate Appointment Service matter

67) Foreign Exchange Management Act FEMA

68) Foreign Trade Policy 2021-26 Proposed

69) Customs Act 1962

70) Narcotic Drugs and Psychotropic Substances Act, 1985 NDPS Act

71) Foreign Trade Development & Regulation Act, 1992

72) How to Search Good Advocate in the Supreme Court of India

73) Sr. Adv Vikas Singh's Interview in Nani Palkhivala Wednesday Law Club

74) Indian Penal Code (I. P. C.)

75) Criminal Procedure Code (Cr. P. C.)

76) Commercial Courts & International Arbitration - by Mr. Jaideep Gupta, Senior Advocate in Nani Palkhivala Wednesday Law Club

77) Sr. Adv Ranji Thomos in Nani Palkhivala Wednesday Law Club

78) Urgent Matters in Supreme Court during vacations

79) 498A Bail Matters in Supreme Court

81) 376 Bail Matters in Supreme Court

82) 302, 304, 307, 308 Bail Matters in Supreme Court

83) 138, 420 Bail Matters in Supreme Court

84) POCSO Act Bail Matters in Supreme Court

85) NDPS Act Bail Matters in Supreme Court

86) What is ED (Enforcement Directorate)?

87) Prevention of Money Laundering Act, 2002 (PMLA Act)

88) Insolvency & Bankruptcy Code- Supreme Court Case Laws. Webinar in Nani Palkhivala Wednesday Law Club

89) What is NCLT & NCLAT?

90) Acquittal from 376- Supreme Court's some case laws in Nani Palkhivala Wednesday Law Club dt 28.7.22

91) Insolvency & Bankruptcy in India

92) Can we file case directly in the Supreme Court?

93) Adv. Anuja Pethia has cleared AOR Exam 2021 with 77% marks - Her interview in Nani Palkhivala Wednesday Law Club

94) Customs Act - Supreme Court Case Laws & Interview of AOR Adv. Anuja Pethia in Nani Palkhivala Law Club.

95) The Uttar Pradesh Public Service Tribunals Act, 1976

96) POCSO Act - Supreme Court Case Laws & Interview of AOR Adv. Shoumendu Mukharji & Adv. Nishant Verma in Nani Palkhivala Law Club.

97) Who Can Trigger CIRP Process Under Insolvency Law of India

98) The Uttar Pradesh Government Servant Discipline and Appeal Rules, 1999

99)CIRP Application Under Sec 7 by FC

100) Information Technology Act 2000

101) Uttar Pradesh Recruitment of Dependants of Government Servants Dying in Harness Rules, 1974

102) Foreign Exchange Management Act 1999 & Supreme Court's Case Laws on FEMA & Leading Case of AOR Exam in Nani Palkhivala Law Club.

103) Arbitration and Conciliation Act 1996 & It's Supreme Court Case Laws in Nani Palkhivala Wednesday Law Club.

104) Narcotic Drugs & Psychotropic Substances Act 1985 (NDPS Act) & It's Supreme Court Case Laws in Nani Palkhivala Wednesday Law Club.

105) Recovery of Debts and Bankruptcy Act 1993

106) Uttar Pradesh Land Revenue Code 2006

107)CIRP Application Under Sec 9 by OC

108)CIRP Application Under Sec 10 by CD

109) Hindu Succession Act, 1956

110) Maharashtra Civil Services Rules, 1981

111) Indian Contract Act, 1872 & Supreme Court's Case Laws" in Nani Palkhiwala Wednesday Law Club

112) Securities and Exchange Board of India Act, 1992 i. e. SEBI Act 1992 & Case Laws on Insiders Trading" in Nani Palkhiwala Wednesday Law Club

113) Moratorium Under Section 14 of IBC, 2016

114) Hindu Marriage Act, 1955

115) Maharashtra Land Revenue Code, 1966

116)64 Leading Cases of AOR Exam Session 1 :- Cases 1 to16 in Nani Palkhiwala Wednesday Law Club

117)64 Leading Cases of AOR Exam Session 2: Cases 17 to 32 in Nani Palkhivala Wednesday Law Club

118)64 Leading Cases of AOR Examination Session 3: Cases 33 to 48 in Nani Palkhivala Wednesday Law Club

119)64 Leading Cases of AOR Exam Session 4: Cases 49 to 64 in Nani Palkhiwala Wednesday Law Club

120) Labour Laws of India: Part 1 - 4 New Labour Law Codes of India

121) New Labour Laws Part 2 The Code on Wages, 2019

122) New Labour Laws Part 3:- The Code on Social Security, 2020

123) Argue in English Fluently & Confidently - Two months online course.

124) SLP Admission in the Supreme Court. 2023 (Hindi)

125) Transfer of Petitions from the Supreme Court (Hindi)

126) Review Petition in the Supreme Court.(Hindi)

127) Recovery of debts from the Company (Hindi)

128) How to search 'Good Insolvency & Bankruptcy Consultant?' (HINDI)

129) Curative Petition in the Supreme Court

130) AFT Appeals in the Supreme Court (HINDI)

131) NCLAT's Appeals in the Supreme Court.

132) Transfer Petition: Which matters can we transfer?

133) SLP Types of SLP in the Supreme court of India (English).

134) Argue in English Fluently and Confidently in the High Court & Supreme Court'.

• • •

List Of Adv. Jayprakash Somani's Published Books

1. Supreme Court of India's Leading Case Laws on 'Insolvency & Bankruptcy Code 2016'
2. Bail Matters – Supreme Court's Latest Leading Case Laws
3. Arbitration Matters- Supreme Court's Latest Leading Case Laws
4. Property Matters - Supreme Court's Latest Leading Case Laws
5. Matrimonial Matters- Supreme Court's Latest Leading Case Laws
6. Election Matters- Supreme Court's Latest Leading Case Laws
7. SEBI Matters- Supreme Court's Latest Leading Case Laws
8. Banking Matters- Supreme Court's Latest Leading Case Laws
9. Service Matters- Supreme Court's Latest Leading Case Laws
10. Contempt of Court Matters- Supreme Court's Latest Leading Case Laws
11. Consumer Protection Matters- Supreme Court's Latest Leading Case Laws
12. Corporate Law- Supreme Court's Latest Leading Case Laws
13. Supreme Court's AOR Exam- Leading Cases
14. Armed Force Tribunal - Supreme Court's Latest Leading Case Laws
15. Acquittal From 376 - Supreme Court's Latest Leading Case Laws
16. Negotiable instrument – Supreme Court's Latest Leading Case Laws
17. Contract Act- Supreme Court's Latest Leading Case Laws
18. Insider trading- Supreme Court's Latest Leading Case Laws
19. Foreign Exchange and Management Act- Supreme Court's Latest Leading Case Laws
20. Income Tax Act- Supreme Court's Latest Leading Case Laws
21. Company Law- Supreme Court's Latest Leading Case Laws
22. Competition & Monopoly Matters- Supreme Court's Latest Leading Case Laws
23. Compassionate Appointment- Service Matters- Supreme Court's Latest Leading Case Laws
24. Compulsory Retirement- Service Matters- Supreme Court's Latest Leading Case Laws
25. Voluntary Retirement- Service Matters- Supreme Court's Latest Leading Case Laws
26. Removal/Dismissal/Termination from Service- Supreme Court's Latest Leading Case Laws

27. Seniority- Service Matter- Supreme Court's Latest Leading Case Laws
28. Promotion- Service Matter- Supreme Court's Latest Leading Case Laws
29. Equal Pay for Equal Work- Service Matter- Supreme Court's Latest Leading Case Laws
30. Condition of Service- Service Matter- Supreme Court's Latest Leading Case Laws
31. Customs Act- Supreme Court's Leading Case Laws
32. Information Technology Act- Supreme Court's Leading Case Laws
33. SEC. 125 CR. P. C.- Supreme Court's Leading Case Laws
34. SEC. 498A OF I. P. C.- Supreme Court's Leading Case Laws
35. MOTOR VEHICLE ACT- Supreme Court's Leading Case Laws
36. CONDITION OF SERVICE- SERVICE MATTER- Supreme Court's Leading Case Laws
37. SUSPENSION- SERVICE MATTER- Supreme Court's Leading Case Laws
38. Reservation in SC, ST, OBC- Service Matter- Supreme Court's Leading Case Laws
39. NARCOTIC DRUGS AND PSYCHOTROPIC SUBSTANCES (NDPS) ACT - Supreme Court of India's Latest Leading Case Laws
40. SEC 302 IPC - Supreme Court of India's Latest Leading Case Laws
41. PROTECTION OF CHILDREN FROM SEXUAL OFFENCES ACT (POCSO) - Supreme Court of India's Latest Leading Case Laws
42. PMLA ACT BAIL MATTERS - Supreme Court of India's Leading Case Laws
43. SEC 376 BAIL MATTERS - Supreme Court of India's Leading Case Laws
44. SEC 302 BAIL MATTERS - Supreme Court of India's Leading Case Laws
45. POCSO ACT BAIL MATTERS - Supreme Court of India's Leading Case Laws
46. JUVENILE JUSTICE ACT- Supreme Court of India's Leading Case Laws
47. TRANSFER OF PROPERTY ACT- Supreme Court of India's Leading Case Laws
48. PROFESSIONAL ETHICS OF ADVOCATES- AOR EXAM- SUPREME COURT'S LEADING CASE LAWS
49. WHITE COLLAR CRIME- SUPREME COURT'S LEADING CASE LAWS
50. SEC 302 BAIL MATTERS- SUPREME COURT'S LEADING CASE LAWS
51. SEC 7 IBC 2016 - SUPREME COURT'S LATEST LEADING CASE LAWS
52. ADVERSE POSSESSION IN PROPERTY MATTER - SUPREME COURT'S LATEST LEADING CASE LAWS
53. FOOD SAFETY AND STANDARD ACT 2006' - SUPREME COURT AND

HIGH COURT's LEADING CASE LAWS

54. ARMED FORCE TRIBUNAL ACT- SUPREME COURT'S LATEST LEADING CASE LAWS

55. ESSENTIAL COMMODITIES ACT 1955- SUPREME COURT'S LATEST LEADING CASE LAWS

56. 'FOREIGN TRADE DEVELOPMENT AND REGULATION ACT'- SUPREME COURT AND HIGH COURT'S LEADING CASE LAWS

57. 'PARTNERSHIP ACT 1932'- SUPREME COURT'S LEADING CASE LAWS

58. 'COTPA ACT 2003' - SUPREME COURT AND HIGH COURT'S LEADING CASE LAWS

59. DOMESTIC VIOLENCE ACT 2005' - SUPREME COURT'S LEADING CASE LAWS

60. 'DOWRY PROHIBITION ACT 1961' - SUPREME COURT'S LATEST CASE LAWS

61. SUPREME COURT'S AOR EXAM- DRAFTING Formates of more than 25 Drafts for AOR Exam Paper 2 - Drafting

Books are available online in India

1. Notion Press: https://notionpress.com/author/jayprakash_somani

2. Amazon: https://www.amazon.in/s?k=jayprakash+somani

3. Flipkart: https://www.flipkart.com/search?q=Jayprakash%20Somani

Books are available online at International Market

4. Amazon International: https://www.amazon.com/s?k=jayprakash+somani

5. Amazon United Kingdom: https://www.amazon.co.uk/s?k=jayprakash+somani

6. E-Books/Kindle edition at National & International Level: https://www.amazon.in/s?k=jaypraksh+somani

• • •

Adv Jayprakash Somani's Online Legal & Import Export Courses

Download our app to get access to our Free Videos, Free Bare Acts, Free Study Material in Legal as well as International Business Regime.

Android App Link ;-https://clpandrea.page.link/cmSm

Ios APp Link :-https://apps.apple.com/us/app/classplus/id1324522260

Login with org code ;- (qywzji)

Web Link ;-https://qywzji.courses.store/

Download App on Google play store - Type

<u>Jayprakash Somani SupremeCourt</u>

Legal Courses :

1. SLP- Bail Matters- Drafting & Successful Arguing in the Supreme Court.

2. SLP- Succession Matters- Drafting & Successful Arguing in the Supreme Court.

3. Legal Vocabulary & its practice pattern to Argue in High Court and Supreme Court / Improve Your Legal English.

4. SLP- Property Matters - Drafting and Successful Arguing in the Supreme Court.

International Business Courses:

1. Agri Products Exports - Scope from India.

2. Textile Exports - Scope from India.

3. Export Import Procedure -Perfect Documentation & It's Management.

4. Jewellery Exports -Scope from India.

5. Export Import Finance Management with LC, ECGC & Venture Capital.

6. Shipping & Logistics in International Business with live links of Ports, ICDs, CHAs etc.

7. International Business Marketing Part 1: Finding Potential & Genuine Buyers for Exports and Suppliers for Imports.

8. International Business Marketing Part 2: Communication Skill to take repeated orders from Potential Buyers.

• • •